Adventure Sports

ROCK
CLIMBING

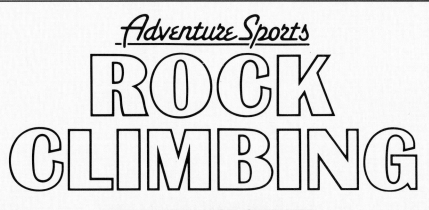

Adventure Sports
ROCK CLIMBING

JOHN BARRY & NIGEL SHEPHERD

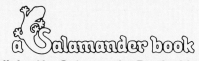

a Salamander book
Published by Salamander Books Limited
LONDON • NEW YORK

A SALAMANDER BOOK

© 1988 Salamander Books Ltd.,
52 Bedford Row,
London, WC1R 4LR,
United Kingdom.

Second Impression

ISBN 0 86101 349 2

Distributed in the UK by
Hodder & Stoughton Services,
P.O. Box 6, Mill Road,
Dunton Green, Sevenoaks,
Kent TN13 2XX.

Edited and designed by: Curtis
Garratt Ltd.
Colour reproductions: Melbourne
Graphics Ltd.
Filmset: SX Composing Ltd.
Printed in Belgium by
Proost International Book
Production, Turnhout.

The authors
John Barry is a former captain of the Royal Marines and
commanded the Mountain and Arctic Warfare Cadre from 1973
to 1976. He was Director of Plas y Brenin, the National Centre
for Mountain Activities. As a leading alpinist he has climbed,
among others, the North Face of the Eiger and has discovered
new routes on mountains the world over, including New
Zealand, Alaska, Norway, and the Himalayas. His other books
include: *Safety in the Mountains, The Great Climbing
Adventure; K2; Savage Mountain, Savage Summer*, and
Improve your Survival Skills.

Nigel Shepherd has been an active amateur and then
professional rock climber since he was sixteen and became
one of Britain's leading climbers during the 1970s. He has
made more than 5000 ascents with some notable firsts and
seconds in Britain, the United States, and New Zealand. He is
also a fully qualified guide and instructor. He recently published
a manual, *Self-rescue Techniques for Climbers and Instructors*
which has been described as '. . . an invaluable little book,
drawing on vast technical knowledge . . .'. He is also a keen
photographer whose work has been published widely in the
climbing press and in brochures.

The illustrator
Mike Woolridge is also a professional mountain guide and has
taken part in climbing expeditions throughout the world for
more than a decade, including climbs in the United Kingdom.

FOREWORD
Rock climbing is now attracting thousands of new followers
each year. Some of these start in the traditional way, and
discover the sport for themselves, while other beginners in
Britain attend one or more of the courses which are now
available almost the length and breadth of the country.
Whichever is your port of entry, a basic book to offer you
advice and information on technique is almost as essential as
to own a rope or a pair of rock boots.
   John Barry and Nigel Shepherd are both well known as
climbing instructors, and their joint experience is such that they
are among the most qualified of authors ever to have prepared
such a book. This book should be enough to get you started
into a sport which is thought by its participants to be
something much more than a mere pastime. For us, it is a way
of life, and a challenging, exciting adventure which can be
enjoyed in some of the most beautiful countryside on Earth.
Thus, I commend this work to you, and congratulate John,
Nigel, and their publisher on a job well done.

Good climbing!

Dennis Gray   British Mountaineering Council

CONTENTS

INTRODUCTION

Man with all his noble qualities . . . still bears in his bodily frame the indelible stamp of his lowly origin
Darwin

In 1969, Tom Patey, doctor, mountaineer, writer and humorist, wrote for *Mountain* magazine an article entitled, 'Apes or Ballerinas?'. It was written in archetypal, good-natured Patey leg-pull. Referring to Darwin's quotation above he wrote: 'If everyone made a point of remembering that, we might be spared a lot of mountain philosophy and psychoanalysis . . . "Why do you climb?" The answer should be apparent to the merest moron. "Because it is the natural thing to do." Climbers are the only genuine primordial humanoids, heirs to a family tradition inherited from hairy arboreal ancestors.'

And Patey is at least half serious – and more than half right. Climbing is natural. We all climbed once. The trouble is that that was a long time ago and most of us have forgotten how to do what we once did naturally; most people except children, that is, who still climb trees – and anything else they can escape their mothers' clutches long

Starting young. Generally, children climb naturally, and, with encouragement, may do well. Learning to climb usually only needs to be remembered.

enough for. On the whole, they climb rather well, too. But for the rest of us, at a depressingly early age we seem to have forgotten. But, even so, in the best case, learning to climb is usually only a process of remembering, or being reminded how to climb, and in the worst it is still only a case of relearning, or being retaught.

This is all good news because it means that the basic skills are in there somewhere. All they need is discovering . . . or, to be precise, rediscovering. So our best advice is to go to it and do what comes naturally. It is an individual's pursuit (the teams are seldom bigger than two) and what comes naturally to you will be, with few exceptions, what is best for you. It is a question of supplementing what comes naturally, not a business of changing it. Patey, still leg-pulling, still at least half serious, had his own views on 'style'.

Where does style come into this . . . Every climber has his own natural 'style', to use the word in its proper context. He inherits it. Climbing instruction, to be of any value, must foster natural style. Try to curb it and you land up in trouble. Try to impose your own style on a 'learner' and you double his difficulties.

The sort of climber I like to watch is the man who knows where he's going, and wastes no time getting there. A latent power and driving force carries him up pitches where no amount of dynamic posturing would do any good. An efficient mountaineer, by this reckoning, need fulfil only three criteria. He must not fall off. He must not lose the route. He must not waste time. Time may be endless on an English outcrop; in the Alps it can mean the difference between life and death.

These are accomplishments to be learnt neither from books nor from other climbers. Although we are all differently proportioned, we all have some natural ability derived from our primitive ancestors, and that's what we need to develop. Which takes us back to the apes. Climbers are conceited characters when you pause to think about it. They liken themselves to Gods, Godesses and Gladiators; tigers, eagles and chamois; craftsmen, gardeners and ballet dancers; and even, in one case at least, to computers! One seldom reads of climbers who resemble apes, chimps or orang-outangs. Comparisons are only odious when too near the bone. You don't teach children to walk . . . they teach themselves. Why, then, teach the descendants of apes to climb . . . They can also be left to teach themselves. But don't expect them to resemble ballet dancers.

So the next time you see a jaded climber at the foot of a cliff, dangle a bunch of bananas from the top. You may be surprised at the energetic response!

This book is intended to supplement practical experience, to encourage, and, we hope, to entertain. There is, however, beyond the basics of style quite a lot to do with climbing that our ancestors never knew for us to forget in the first place: such as ropes and knots, footwear (I think they went barefoot) and equipment, and protection (our ancestors' falls may have been infrequent but they were usually fatal and that is to be avoided!), and of other climbing areas the whole world over (our ancestors were a parochial lot).

This book offers some advice on how to take the first steps; an introduction to what is hoped will be a game of a lifetime.

An instructor and student enjoying a first climb. Perhaps this will be the start of a lifetime's pleasure for this novice.

A summer evening's climb high above the Llanberis Pass, North Wales. Climbing can take you into some stunning scenery.

CHAPTER 1

THOSE FIRST STEPS

You can begin right away; you do not need any equipment other than a pair of trainers. Find a low, friendly boulder, one that has easy-angled facets and abounds with cracks and ledges of all sizes. Make sure, too, that the ground below is flat and soft with no threatening rocks to cause injury should you slip off. And do not go alone; take someone with you to act as a spotter whose role it is to see that you do not topple over backwards in the event of an unexpected fall. There is no need to go high. As high as you can comfortably jump from will be fine. On a boulder, go up and down and across; the footage will soon add up, as will the experience and fun. On walls, make distance horizontally – you need only be a metre or so above the ground. Then experiment with the feet (the feet go first – everyone's feet and legs are far stronger than their hands and arms). So use your feet as much as possible. Try them front-on on whatever holds you have found. Then sideways – trainers, and indeed most modern rock boots (*see* pages 28-9) work best sideways on small holds. Then try the holds you did not see at first; the small ones and the ones that slope so much that they did not look like holds. Discover how much friction you have; how little you need. Discover, too, how little you need hands on less than vertical rock especially where there are good footholds; try no hands at all, test your balance. Make a game of it. If your boulder, rock or wall is too lilberally equipped with holds, try missing out a few; or if it has been sparingly supplied, keep at it until you have solved the problem: a foot this way, or that way, or perhaps over there, with the hands here, or there. If pulling with the hands does not work, try pushing (which is less tiring anyway – everyone I know can do many more push-ups than pull-ups). Try anything and everything that comes with your head (or feet and hands); remember what worked and when and how. Build up a library of experience – a ready reference at instant recall. Self-taught lessons are seldom forgotten. In the end, the only important difference between climbers is those who get up and those who do not. The illustrations show a few of the more common holds.

BALANCE HOLDS, BALANCE CLIMBING, AND SLABS

The 'look no hands' climbing style is sparing of strength and energy. Everyone has balance to some

Right: Good balance and confidence are needed.

Below: A low, friendly boulder, South Island, New Zealand.

degree but there are climbers with good balance and those with bad. Good balance is useful on slabs (that is, rock up to an angle of about 60 degrees where most, if not all, the weight may be kept on the feet, the hands doing little more than adding reassurance and an extra point of balance. On such a climb, a foothold may be little more than the merest lessening in the general angle or the smallest of cracks or protuberances that lends the boot enough friction to defy gravity and bear your weight. Generally speaking, the steeper a climb the more the hands are used to supplement balance. To some, the economical use of the hands (and arms) is instinctive, while others have to concentrate to relax, and make a conscious lack of effort. To begin with, most climbers hang on just a little harder than is necessary to maintain balance or to defy gravity, but practice will make nearer to perfect. Games can be made of balancing, too – on planks, on fence tops, or even, as a balance training aid, on a rope or wire stretched between two trees no more than about ¾ metre (about 2 feet) off the ground.

On your friendly boulder you will soon discover how well your feet work and on what angles and in what conditions. Greasy, grassy, or wet, limestone slabs do not offer the friction that bone-dry, rough gritstone slabs afford. (In any case, limestone is not characterized by slabs; it tends to form vertically or horizontally.) By the same token, all angles being equal, the rougher the rock, the better the friction. Cornish granite, or the granite of Mount Buffalo, Victoria, Australia, or that of the Etive Slabs near Glencoe in Scotland, offer considerable friction. The gritstone of the Peak District of Derbyshire is more compact and affords less – although it is still

On small footholds, use the inside edge of the toes. This is 'Scarlet Runner', an E4,5c climb on slate in North Wales.

Relying on friction for the feet. Smooth, holdless, but rough granite, Whitehorse Ledge, New Hampshire, United States.

good rock for friction (as generations of grazed arms, legs, and backsides have testified). The Idwal Slabs of Cwm Idwal, North Wales, are perhaps the best-known beginners' slabs in Britain. The Idwal Slabs are composed of rhyolite, and must once have provided excellent friction. Now, the padding of millions of feet later, those rocks are smoother than nature intended –

although it is still a great place to pad and to learn about slabs and friction and climbing and fun. Similarly, the slabs of White Horse near North Conway, New Hampshire are good for beginners.

At the meeting place of gravity and friction, slabs are far from beginners fare. There are very hard slab routes on Derbyshire grit, for example, where the difference be-

tween up and down can be the pounding of a nervous heart; and there are still other slabs, such as those of the Apron in Yosemite Valley, California, where to stop to think or to rest is to slide inexorably downwards, and where to go up is to keep moving, to keep padding, frictioned foot to frictioned foot. Go gently angled to begin and you will quickly learn the balance-and-slab trade, and that which will and will not make a foothold. Modern 'sticky' soled boots (page 29) make a big difference on slabs, but your trainers will do to begin. Just one tip – do not lean into the rock. Physics decrees that you earn more friction (and enjoyment) standing more or less upright, that is, comfortably in balance. Now let us look at some specific techniques.

JAMS AND JAMMING

Sometimes a piece of rock may not present obvious hand holds, but if there are cracks, even though they may be smooth sided, the knowing climber will find ample purchase by using a technique generally known as jamming. Experienced climbers grow misty eyed on the subject of jams: an ancient art form honed to painful perfection on roughest gritstone; the battlescars of their apprenticeship livid on the backs of beerglass-filled hands to prove it. If you believe those gritstone graduates, then jamming was invented on (and for) grit. That may be true. It is certain, however, that the jamming of fingers, hands, fists, and feet is, once perfected – and it takes a lot of perfecting – a secure and efficient way, indeed sometimes the only way, of climbing cracks. There are vertical and even overhanging cracks that, though bereft of the merest hold for hand or foot, are eminently jammable. Once mastered, the jam becomes a friendly thing, a talking point: 'there's a really good jam over the bulge'; a target, 'go for that jam'; a sanctuary, 'keep going, you can rest at the jam'; or a lifesaver, 'good job I got the jam, I was in trouble'. There are many different kinds of jam, as well as jams for most bits of the body, including, in extremes, the

Below left: No grips for the hands here! The climber must rely on jammed hands and feet. The right foot is thrown out for balance.

Below and bottom: A two-finger jam, secure but slightly painful. The fingers are crossed for comfort and to create a wider profile.

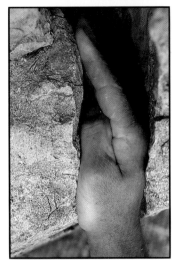

backside and the head! This is not, however, what 'climbing with your head' usually means.

Jams for the hands

Do not forget that one person's finger jam may be another's off-hand, while an off-hand for another may be a full hand jam for his or her partner; much depends on the size of your hand. Try them all on your friendly boulder, with finger this way and that; with thumbs up and down, tucked into the palm and open; with arms flexed this way, that way; with body leaning to left, or to right. Be imaginative. With only a little experience, the jam will soon be a natural part of your repertoire, although awkward cracks will always demand a certain amount of in-situ exploration and experimentation. And do not forget the feet – even on the steepest of jamcracks, there is often something for them somewhere. Look around, that jamcrack is not the whole world – although it sometimes is the only bit of the world that you are conscious of – and even half a foothold can take a lot of weight and tension off a jam.

Finger jams

Sometimes very painful and slightly worrying, finger jams offer a secure attachment to narrow cracks. The most secure are where the fingers are inserted up to the knuckle.

Off-hand jams

These are jams between the finger and full hand size.

Jams for the feet

Footwork is important and, if there are no holds for the feet on either side of your hand jamcrack, then it

Top left: A more secure finger jam. The hand is twisted to create a 'camming' action.

Above left and left: The 'perfect' hand jam. Place the open hand into the crack, then push your thumb into the palm of your hand. Push your fingertips against the side of the crack, hang back, and enjoy the security!

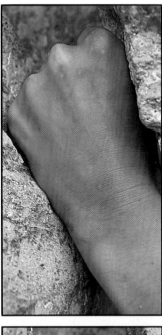

Top: A fist jam, outside view. The use of jams should come naturally.

Above: An inside view of the same jam. The thumb is pushed into the palm to stretch the skin tight and create a wider profile. This means less painful jams.

Top: A toe jam. The foot is twisted for better jamming.

Above: A foot jam. Friction is won at both heel and toe thanks to the boot's wrap-round rubber rand.

Right: An off-width. Too wide for hand and foot jams.

may be possible to jam with the feet – or at least a foot – too.

Off-widths

This is the term (of American origin) given to cracks that are too wide to jam with the fists, but too narrow to get the whole body into. Indeed, it is American climbers who have perfected the techniques needed to climb the off-width cracks with which geology has blessed, or cursed, the United States. Of one of Britain's most notorious off-widths, Right Eliminate at Curbar, it is written in the guide book:

Right Eliminate E3

Technically impossible to grade. The energy expended in each ascent could light Sheffield for a week. Follow the wide crack making two moves up and one down until the ordeal is over. Strangely tempting.

In truth they tend towards strenuousness. Brute strength, short levers, and a raging-bull approach will sometimes stand in office of technique – sometimes. One worrying aspect of off-widths is that protection is characteristically sparse, sometimes non-existent, so that, if your energy runs out before the climb you may be faced with an abrasive slither – at the least.

Resting while jamming

Even for the most adept, a long jam-crack is likely to be a strenuous

Left: A master of off-widths at work. American climbers have perfected this art because of the demands of their rock.

Above: Sometimes a resting position may not be obvious. Here the climber is hanging off a jammed knee.

stopping to try for a rest, or retreating to the nearest runner, or the ground (whichever comes first!).

If off-widths sound less than attractive then that is because most climbers find them so. Indeed, there are very good climbers who would climb a long way to avoid them. Try them though. Some bodies seem to be naturally tuned for off-widths.

PRESSURE TECHNIQUES

Chimneys

Chimneys are cracks that are wide enough to accommodate the entire climber. The slimmest chimneys – squeeze chimneys as they are called – are not, therefore, necessarily chimneys for the fattest! A comfortably wide chimney is best climbed by 'backing and footing'; that is, back on one wall, feet on the other, hands low, and the palms of the hands pressing.

Chimneys are not usually anything like as strenuous to climb as

business. Spy out likely resting places before you set out, and rest on your feet as much as you can. Experiment. Ways of resting are not always immediately obvious but, with experience, you will find them more readily. If there are no footholds at which a rest may be won, and if you need a rest urgently, then try for a good jam with one hand and lower on to it until the arm of the jammed hand is straight. This way the bones bear the strain. A bent arm allows no rest because that arm's muscles are still doing all the work. While resting on the straightened arm, dangle the other arm loose and low, and perhaps shake it to encourage oxygen back into tired muscles. Alternate arms until both are improved – and away you go again. But do not expect that your arms will recover completely; at best, they will only improve. There is quite a fine calculation to be done between rushing for the top, or

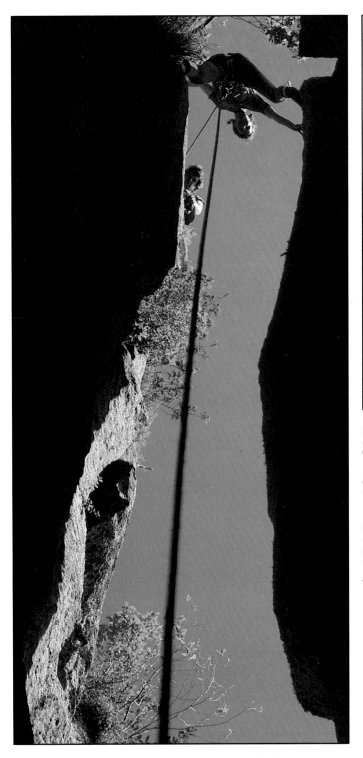

Left: A chimney climb. 'Tibia Chimney', a grade 16 climb at Whanganui Bay, New Zealand.

Above: Climbing a narrow chimney using pressure holds.

Right: You do not always need to save back and foot technique for chimneys. Here it is demonstrated well in a more open situation.

off-widths and, once the various chimneying ploys are mastered, it is possible to progress with speed and economy, and to rest as often as you like.

Laybacking
Laybacking is a useful technique for arêtes, corners with cracks, and cracks offset in walls. These are climbs where every move is a layback, sometimes without respite and, if they are steep, they are stren-

uous. Other climbs will sport a particular set of holds that, in their juxtaposition, suggest that a single layback move is the quickest way to gain a little distance – these are sometimes called layaway moves. On a sustained layback, avoid bringing the feet too close to the hands; this increases the strain taken by the arms. Keep the arms more-or-less straight so that bones rather than muscles are working and, as when jamming, if nature has provided a foothold, use it. Placing protection 'on layback' is awkward, and sometimes that old decision has to be made quickly, 'do I use the energy that I have left to place a runner (*see* page 47), or to go for it?'.

Right, below, and far right: A sequence to show the laybacking technique. Always make sure that you look for footholds. Continuous laybacking is strenuous.

Mantelshelves and mantelling

A mantelshelf move, as shown in the photographs, is necessary if you are confronted with a shelf of rock (the mantelshelf) below and above which there are no holds that may otherwise be used to gain that shelf. Wide shelves are easier to mantel over than narrow shelves. Having decided that a mantel is the method by which a particular problem is to be reduced, an energetic launch will help to produce the momentum to get most of your body weight (and with it your centre of gravity) over the hand, or hands. Would-be mantellers often fail to finish the move because they have not launched boldly enough. If the edge is good, or if you have a runner nearby, you will usually be able to have a second try although the failure will have cost some of your energy and perhaps something of your nerve too.

Top left, bottom left, below, and right: A sequence showing the mantelshelf technique. Once again, footholds and a bold launch are important.

Left: Climbing a corner by bridging across with the feet and pressure holds with the hands. 'Bircheff/Williams' route, Middle Cathedral, Yosemite Valley, USA.

Above: The widest of wide bridging moves!

Bridging

Bridging is the most efficient way to climb corners and wide chimneys and, even when the technique is not used to make progress, it may be a good way of winning a rest; a foot thrown out to a bridge often enables the climber's weight to be taken on the legs, relieving the arms and perhaps allowing one of them, even both sometimes, to be dangled in rest. Bridging may also tame what would otherwise have been a stren-

uously overhanging groove. The more supple you are, the better you will bridge, and the longer your legs, the wider will you bridge. It is always necessary to have footholds to bridge; enough pressure can be exerted on spaced feet to maintain a position from which more bridging moves may be made.

While bridging with the legs, the hands can be used in most of the ways that have already been discussed: jamming, layawaying, pushing, palming, and even bridging with the arms, too.

Other considerations

Overhangs

Even when they are liberally supplied with generously proportioned holds, overhangs tend to be strenuous. Try to climb using just enough

strength to maintain position and, in some cases, momentum. Conserve energy by using the feet as much as possible. It is surprising how much you can benefit from the friction of one foot on vertical, holdless rock even on a straight, two-armed pull up. On harder, steep climbs, it is sometimes necessary to lock off to make the next move. Undeniably, this is a strenuous procedure and, although it is unlikely to be necessary on first outings, it is something that may be practised in safety on that friendly boulder.

Roofs

A roof is an overhang, edging towards the horizontal. Roofs vary in size from an eave of a few centimetres to great cantilevers which are metres wide. Even the smallest roofs need holds on which to pull

over. Big roofs need big holds, or a crack running through in which to jam and, with any luck, place protection. It is unlikely that you will encounter anything but the simplest of roofs in your first forays but again, it is something that you could practise on a boulder or at the local climbing wall.

Face climbing

When applied to rock climbing, a face usually means a wall of rock, steeper than 60 degrees or so, that lacks any other distinguishing feature such as a groove, a crack, or a chimney line. Face climbs often feel more exposed than other kinds

Far left top and bottom: Overhangs require plenty of strength . . .

Left: . . . but roofs require more! 'Quietus', a classic roof climb on Stanage Edge, Derbyshire.

Below: A very hard face climb. 'The Electric Cool-Aid Acid Test' an E4, 6c climb at Pen Trwyn, North Wales.

Above: A technique quite easily accomplished for making use of very small finger holds.

Above: A small 'pocket' finger hold. Be ready to make use of such small holds.

Above: A pinchgrip, just one of your armoury of moves for face climbing.

Right: An undercling. Holds such as these allow the climber to adopt a fairly restful position provided that there are good footholds. It also allows one to make a long reach for a handhold should it be necessary.

of route; steep, featureless walls concentrate the mind wonderfully. There may be, however, ample holds and more than adequate protection; it is a matter of discovery, and of experience. The smallest cracks, holes, and flakes will often accommodate modern protection devices (*see* Chapter 3) and your full armoury of moves can often be brought to bear even on faces which are apparently lacking in features or lines of weakness: bridging in the merest of grooves, in the suggestion of corners; layaways on bumps, knobs, edges; jams here and there; pinchgrips. Be ready and willing to use them all. Limestone is rock particularly given to walls which, on first sight, appear to be featureless, if not holdless. Closer inspection, however, will often reveal solution holes sized for anything from one finger to entire arms (in the Gorge du Verdon, the French call these *gouttes d'eau*). So the message is that what looks blank, especially on limestone, is not necessarily lost.

As in all climbing, use the feet as much as possible. Lower limb and hip mobility will bring into range a greater selection of holds and possibilities, while, generally speaking, the feet are used turned sideways so that the stiffer profile, the edge of

the boot (inside or outside) is brought to bear on the hold. Most footwork involves the front inside edge.

Other ploys and tricks

Arm bar
This is useful at odd times when nothing else fits.

Knee bar
This is hardly an everyday hold but one which, when found, allows both hands to be released for a rest. Unless you have skin to spare it is as well not to knee bar in shorts.

Heel hooks
Heel hooks are mandatory when making films about rock climbing. Then they must always be performed in as lurid a pair of lurex tights as the rainbow allows, and sporting a dangling chalkbag against the backdrop of a cobalt-blue sky. Films apart, it is an occasionally useful way in which to relieve the arms of some body-weight. Sometimes, though rarely, it is the best way of gaining the next hold.

'Dynos' (from 'dynamic', meaning movement)
There are times when a hold seems to be beyond reach. Try sinking slightly and then rising by pushing with the legs and pulling with whichever hand has the hold. The free hand grabs for the dyno. It works well as long as the hold for which you are 'dyno-ing' actually exists. It is worth being certain beforehand – and this is not always easy. The youngest and brightest sparks have now perfected the 'double-dyno' in which the dynamics are too awesome to contemplate. A 'double-dyno' is two 'dynos' in succession. Anyway, if you can 'double-dyno, you have advanced well beyond the level of this page.

Top left: An arm bar is a useful hold to use when there is no alternative.
Left: A heel hook. While it is a little 'flashy', this does relieve quite a lot of strain off the arms.

CHAPTER 2

BASIC EQUIPMENT

Joe Brown and his friends are reputed to have begun their climbing days wearing pumps, with Joe's mother's washing-line for a rope. This story has not yet been confirmed by Mrs Brown (senior) as far as I know. Perhaps it is better that way; there is romance in the notion. Fortunately for mothers who love their offspring but unfortunately for the pocket, climbing is no longer like that. Climbing shops are piled, mountains high, with gear; and it is all better, safer, lighter, and brighter. It is also more expensive.

To begin with, on your very first manoeuvres on boulders and on your first scrambles on first routes, you get away with some old clothes and a pair of trainers. Soon, though,

A selection of equipment for a three-day 'Big Wall' climb.

you will want to match your growing ability with better and more equipment. Soon, too, that same better equipment will have you climbing more safely, more enjoyably, and probably better. If your budget does not stretch to the full range of appropriate gear in one shopping spree, then you will have to decide what ought to come first. Your order of priority might be: rock boots; rope; harness; belay brake; karabiner; slings and nuts; and then whatever takes your fancy – if you have any money left. If money is no object, that list will get you going in grand style in one fell purchase and see you through your first year into the bargain, although you can go on adding accoutrements, and accessories to those accoutrements, for ever more. Let us deal with the basics, though not necessarily in the suggested order.

BOOTS

Rock climbers spend most of their time on their feet, and feet are the principal source of friction. Therefore, a good pair of rock boots is probably the most important part of the entire ensemble. Happily, the days are gone when climbers shod themselves in great leather boots soled with savage rows of nails, or equally cumbersome moulded and cleated rubber-soled clodhoppers, or socks over pumps to encourage them to greater friction when the rock was wet. Gone, too, are the days when only one lightweight rock boot, the once ubiquitous 'EB' was available. These days, we are spoilt for choice of rock boots which are a lot better at the job for which they were designed – climbing dry rock – than any of their predecessors. No-one climbs in the wet anymore if

they can avoid it. This is probably a good thing, too. Go into a well-stocked climbing retailer and you can expect to see ten or more different models of rock boot on offer. They will all work tolerably well; most will work very well. There is no need to worry too much about which model you select.

Go for the most comfortable pair, and possibly then the cheapest. The average rock boot lasts the average climber about two years. By the time they are worn out, you will know a lot more about the sport, you will have developed all manner of preferences and prejudices, and you can spend happy hours contemplating your second pair of rock boots. A

A selection of rock climbing boots. Choose the most comfortable.

fairly recent development is the 'sticky sole'. These soles are made of a softer – and less rugged – rubber, that is, they afford more friction. Do not settle for anything less. They make an enormous difference and there is no point in handicapping your early days for the sake of cash.

The best footwear to take you to and from the crag is a pair of trainers. Save your rock boots for the rock. They will last longer that way and, in any case, they work better when the soles are clean and dry. When fitting your boots in the shop, wear whatever thickness of sock you are likely to use on the climb. I know climbers who wear no socks (cool on cold days) and climbers who wear thick socks (hot on warm days). It is unlikely that one good-fitting pair of rock boots (and they ought to be a close, comfortable fit) will accommodate the difference,

even though unlined boots have a tendency to stretch. Perhaps the best, and most usual, compromise is a pair of thin socks. But it does not matter very much.

ROPE

Forget the washing line, or hemp or manila, or hawser-laid nylon Today's climbing rope is universally kernmantel, the name given to nylon ropes constructed with an inner, usually plaited, strength-giving core that is protected by an outer, woven sheath. Kernmantel ropes come in all lengths (the core filaments are of continuous construction and have no joins) and in a variety of diameters, the most common of which are 5, 7, 9, and 11 millimetre (roughly between ⅜ and ½ inch). Each diameter has its place, but for rock climbing, either a single

11-millimetre or a double 9-millimetre rope is considered essential. (*See* Chapter 4 for ropework.) Recently, a new generation of 8.8-millimetre ropes have been gaining popularity over the slightly heavier 9-millimetre ropes. When you buy a rope, make sure it carries a UIAA (Union Internationale des Associations d'Alpinisme) sticker which will also label the rope a 'single', 11-millimetre; or '½' rope, 9-millimetre and therefore intended for use with a second 9-millimetre rope. The most common lengths are 45 and 50 metres (150 and 165 feet). The difference in length matters little; the difference in price might.

Climbing ropes are immensely strong. A 9-millimetre rope has a breaking strain of about 1500 kilograms (3300 pounds) and an 11-millimetre about 2000 kilograms (4400 pounds). Most of this strength is derived from the rope's elasticity, which comes from two sources. The core filaments themselves are inherently elastic, but as much as two-thirds of a rope's stretch is given by the way in which the filaments are woven together. This weave also governs other aspects of a rope's behaviour – flexibility, feel, softness, how or if it kinks, resistance to abrasion, strength over edges, and the like. The perfect rope does not exist because many desirable qualities are mutually exclusive, and the manufacturer is faced with settling for compromises. A stiff rope, for example, will be resistant to kinking but may not feel good. A soft rope may handle pleasantly but is likely to abrade

more quickly than a hard one. The one quality that is never compromised is elasticity, for it is this that enables a rope to absorb the energy of a fall and which gives the rope its strength. The same elasticity also spares the arrested climber a body-wracking jolt.

You need not, though, be greatly worried by your choice of a first rope. Any rope with a UIAA label will be a good one. You have only to decide between 9-millimetre ropes used doubly, or 11-millimetre ones used singly. A single 'eleven' is cheaper than two 'nines', although many people own only one 'nine', relying on the partner to supply the second. Practically, an 'eleven' will see you safely and satisfactorily through your first year or so; then, as you become more ambitious, you may benefit from the advantages afforded by a double 'nine' system: longer abseils (*see* Chapter 5) and less rope drag (*see* page 58). For your first steps, the choice is not a crucial one and price may decide the day.

Care of rope
Nylon ropes do not rot but they are prone to other forms of damage. It is worth looking after your rope. Your life may depend on it and, in any case, they are expensive.

Damage by falls
A severe fall may damage a rope in one, or more, of three ways.
1. The rope may be stretched taut over an edge or jam in thin cracks which, if sharp or abrasive enough, could cut into it, or even through it.

Above left: Rope for climbing. Today's rope is always kernmantel.

Above: The construction of a kernmantel rope. The detail of construction may vary with manufacturer but all are essential similar.

Take care to route the rope away from edges and clear of thin cracks.
2. Nylon melts at a very low temperature – about 220°C (428°F). A moving, weighted rope running across the same point of a static rope for more than a few seconds will easily generate such a temperature. When belaying (page 47), ensure that any rope that is likely to move in the event of a fall is not likely to run across any of the non-moving rope involved in anchoring to the rock.
3. A very hard fall will stretch the nylon filaments beyond the point of full recovery, and much of the rope's capacity to absorb energy will be lost. Unfortunately, there is no hard-and-fast definition of what constitutes a hard fall, but most manufacturers recommend that, after a fall of factor 2, or more (page 64), you should replace your rope (and possibly forsake climbing in favour of snooker).

Localized damage
Falling stones can nick or cut ropes. Check yours from time to time by running your hand and eye along its length. On dirty crags, grit may work its way through the sheath where it will damage the filaments whenever

Above and right: Coiling a rope. It is important to ensure that there are no tangles in the rope prior to coiling. Begin from the middle of the rope and lap each loop over the hand. Once there is about 1.5 metres (5 feet) left, begin wrapping the spare around the loops (top right). Finally pass a loop through the main hank and tuck the rope ends through it. The rope can be carried in a rucksack or in the manner illustrated far right.

the rope is exercised vigorously. Standing on a rope does not do it any good either. Dirty or gritty ropes are best washed in fresh water with a mild detergent, and dried by hanging out loosely in an airy, naturally heated place, away from direct sunlight. Ultra-violet light inflicts considerable damage on a nylon rope; window glass is no protection, so do not leave ropes in windows, and avoid those that have been displayed in shop windows.

Normal use will eventually abrade the fibres of the sheath of any rope; rough rock, such as granite or gritstone, will do this more than smoother rock, such as some limestones. There is no 'litmus test' for determining when a rope's useful

life has ended. As a very rough guide, a rope that has been regularly used for weekend climbing but is otherwise undamaged should be 'retired' after about two years. Ropes used less often than that will last proportionately longer, provided that they have been looked after and stored carefully, that is, in a dark, dry, well-ventilated place, well away from acids or oils that might weaken or stain the filaments.

The boot of a car is not a good home for a safe rope.

Kinking and coiling

Most kernmantel ropes kink; some more than others. Care in coiling helps (see page 55) to keep a rope free from kinks – and kinks can be infuriating. If your rope begins to tangle, try dragging it through grass or allowing it to dangle over a drop so that the kinks and tangles fall out.

TAPE

Nylon tape for climbing is con-structed in a flat or tubular webbing weave in widths between 10 and 25 millimetres (²⁄₅ to 1 inch). Flat tape is usually available in two thicknesses, standard and super. Tubular tape is usually softer than flat tape, and 'feels' and handles well. It holds knots poorly, however, and is more prone to damage by abrasion and cuts than stiffer, tougher, and tighter flat tape. Most retailers sell tape by the metre so that you can fashion your own tape slings (page 43), as well as a selection of prestitched slings and quick draws. A sewn sling is stronger at the join than a knotted one of the same tape and a sewn join is neater and smaller than a knot. If price is the governing fac-tor, then homemade slings are cheaper and, properly tied with a tape knot (page 62), perfectly satis-factory. Slings may also be made from climbing rope, also available in metre lengths, in 5, 7, 9, and 10-mil-limetre (³⁄₅ to ½-inch) diameters. Slings of tape and rope should be treated with the same care and sub-ject to the same inspections as your climbing rope.

HARNESS

There was a time when climbers tied the climbing rope directly to their waist. Happily, those days are gone. Almost all modern rock climbers use a sit-harness of one type or another. There is a vast and colourful array available and preferences are based as much on prejudice as anything else. A sit-harness has many advan-tages over tying on directly to the rope: it is a more convenient way in which to join rope and torso; it is much more comfortable to fall in – and less stressful on the waist as that fall is arrested, because the big muscles of the buttocks and thighs bear the brunt of the shock (com-pared to the cheese-wire effect of a rope tied directly to the waist); and a harness offers convenient loops in which to clip runners and other paraphernalia (page 47).

Most harnesses are made of wide tape sewn into shape. All have an adjustable waist, the fastening of

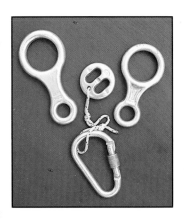

Left: An assortment of nylon tape used by climbers. Treat tape with care.

Above: A belay plate and pear-shaped karabiner, and two types of descendeur.

Below: A set of basic equipment for rock climbing. This should have you climbing safely.

which is important: make sure you have it right (page 51); some have adjustable leg loops and these can be advantageous – legs clad in several winter thicknesses are very different in circumference to summer legs bared to the sun.

A rock climbing harness should be comfortable; you may wear it for hours at a time with several kilos of rope and gear hanging from it. It is worth trying them on in the shop before deciding which one to buy. Check, too, that you have the correct size. Sizes of harnesses that do not have adjustable leg loops are more critical than those that do. Familiarizing yourself with a new harness at home can save embarrassing minutes of discovery and disentanglement at the foot of a climb. They are all fairly straightforward, but, if you really try, you can usually manage to gird yourself inside out or, with a greater effort, upside down!

Full body harness, or combinations of sit- and chest harnesses, are popular in Europe although are rarely seen in Britain, the United States, or Australasia. The big advantage of this sort of harness is that the shock load of a fall is distributed over an even wider area and, because the arrested climber always remains in an upright position, there is less likelihood of head and rock colliding during a fall. These undoubted advantages notwithstanding, British and American climbers have almost unanimously voted for sit-harnesses with their backsides, eschewing the safer body harness in favour of the greater freedom and comfort afforded by a sit-harness.

BELAY PLATE

It is possible to belay and hold a fall with body and hands. That is the way it used to be done. Today, however, some kind of belay plate is the all-but-universally accepted method of belaying (*see* page 52) and of holding falls. It is easier and safer – for both the belayer and the belayed. They are delightfully simple devices – little more than a small plate of metal with one slot (for a single rope) or two slots (double

ropes) cut in them. Correctly used in conjunction with a large, pear-shaped locking or screw-gate karabiner (*see* below and page 52) and with a climbing rope, they are nearly foolproof.

A short length of accessory cord [10 centimetres (4 inches) or so] will keep the belay plate and its karabiner within working distance when in use, and also make it more difficult to lose or drop. Belay plates can also be used to abseil (*see* page 74) although, if you anticipate thousands of metres of abseiling, you might prefer to use a descendeur (*see* page 73).

DESCENDEURS

These are devices used for descending ropes, that is, abseiling or, rapelling (*see* page 73). The most commonly used device is the 'figure of eight'.

KARABINERS

There are two broad categories of karabiner: locking and ordinary. Ordinary karabiners ('krabs' in climbers' jargon) are also referred to as snaplinks. The gatekeeper of a locking krab may be secured by either a screw sleeve or by a spring-loaded sleeve. Modern karabiners are made of aluminium alloy and forged into approximately D shapes with spring-loaded gates. A D-shaped karabiner is stronger than other shapes because applied weight is directed on to the side away from the gate – the gate always being the weakest point on any karabiner.

For mosts tasks, climbers use snaplinks. The place for locking karabiners is when there is a chance that the gate may be accidentally sprung open and where such a chance happening could be dangerous. Therefore, they are used chiefly for belaying and abseiling and, while a large D-shaped locking karabiner performs these jobs satisfactorily, a pear-shaped karabiner does them better because it provides more room for two 9-millimetre ropes to run side-by-side.

A large pear-shaped karabiner also accommodates single or

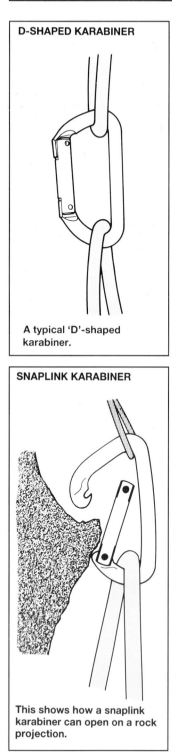

D-SHAPED KARABINER

A typical 'D'-shaped karabiner.

SNAPLINK KARABINER

This shows how a snaplink karabiner can open on a rock projection.

double Italian hitches (*see* page 62) and allows them room to be operated smoothly. There are times when this is useful. Whatever type and whatever shape of locking karabiner you select, check that it is UIAA approved and that it has an advertised breaking strain of at least 2500 kilograms (5500 pounds).

Snaplinks, as their name suggests, are faster to deploy than locking karabiners, and are designed for use where the chance of the gate being sprung is unlikely or unimportant, that is, for clipping the climbing rope into running belays (*see* Chapter 4). A leader may carry as many as thirty – so that the weight of individual karabiners is worth considering. Most snaplinks will be rated around 2200 kilograms (4840 pounds) breaking strain, although recently, lighter models rated between 1800 and 2000 kilograms (4000 to 4400 pounds) depending on the make, are gaining in popularity. These super lightweights, weighing as little as 40 grams (1½ oz) are not as safe as their slightly heavier, 2200-rated cousins – and they do not carry the UIAA stamp of approval. They have been known to fail under severe falls and you should consider carefully whether you need to save those grams. The chances are that, until you are climbing Extremes (*see* page 112), you do not. An advertised breaking strain of 1800 to 2000 kilograms (4000 to 4400 pounds) is, in ideal circumstances, far greater than any load a karabiner is likely to be subjected to, but these figures are earned with the gate closed. All karabiners are much weakened when the gate is open. This is especially true of the lightweight variety. It occasionally happens that a karabiner is loaded by a fall with the gate open; for example, when it is pressed against a projecting ribbon of rock or an edge.

In these rare circumstances, the margin of safety in a lightweight karabiner is narrow. Until your experience enables you to gauge these margins fairly accurately, and certainly to begin with, it seems prudent to take out the better insurance of UIAA stamped snaplinks which are more likely to guarantee safety.

Care of karabiners

Contrary to traditional wisdom, dropping karabiners short distances does them no harm – although dropping them and failing to retrieve them will inflict considerable damage on your pocket! Salt water and sea spray, however, corrode aluminium alloy, with alarming rapacity and rapidity. Inspect your rack a few days after climbing on a sea cliff and you will soon spot evidence of salt corrosion. A periodic rinse in fresh water will sort this out. If you should drop your rack, or yourself, in the sea, be sure to give all your gear a good freshwater rinse. Recalcitrant karbiner gates can be effectively restored with a squirt of a silicone-based spray lubricant.

HELMET

It cannot be denied that helmets make climbing safer. A helmet affords protection to the head in two ways: against stonefall damage from above and against head injuries from a collision with the rock face during a fall, or with the ground after a fall. Most climbers I know only wear a helmet for rock climbing (as distinct from winter climbing or alpinism) when they feel there is a threat of falling stones, perhaps dislodged by passing animals or by fellow climbers. It is still a good idea to wear a helmet, however. But it is yet another encumbrance, it makes a hot day hotter and – well, in truth, most of us, ignoring our own better judgement, just do not bother.

Helmets are especially good for beginners because a fall on an easy, low-angled climb full of ledges, slabs, and boulders involves a downward journey that is potentially far more damaging to the skull than a short plop from some modern overhanging horror of an E8 (*see* page 112) where there may not be much more to argue with than thin air. There are lightweight helmets, too, so that if you can not bear the weight and discomfort of the full-weight variety (and they are not really that uncomfortable) you may be ready to settle for a lightweight compromise affording at least a measure of skull protection. Hel-

hour cooling off while your partner follows, and a further half-hour sliding into a deep freeze while he leads the next pitch. On the other hand, there is nothing worse than being too hot, although you can always take a pullover off and tie it around your waist, or tuck it into your harness, or agree an arrangement whereby the leader travels light, and the second brings up the sweaters. And you cannot put on what you have not got.

Thus, it is anything from shorts and bare tops on a really hot day to fibrepile or 'thermofleece' top and bottom on a cool day. As long as the clothing allows free movement of the arms and legs, it matters little. A light wind makes a warm day cool, a cool day cold. A simple, light, cheap, cotton windproof will make all those days more comfortable – and you will climb better and more enjoyably as a result. A spare pullover, mitts, and a balaclava are no bad thing on mountain crags, or on any crag far from the road.

A mountain rock climb in North Wales. On such climbs, climbers will often carry all their spare clothing and equipment with them on the route.

mets are subject to UIAA criteria (based on strength and resilience) so that, if you intend to invest in one, you might as well buy an approved model. Most helmets are made of a mixture of fibreglass and resin, some are of plastic, and a few of carbonfibre.

GEAR FOR PROTECTION

Information on the variety of equipment used to protect the leader will be found from page 38.

Rucksack
A rucksack is a useful, rather than an essential accessory; it is especially useful if the crag of your choice is some distance from the road. Many equally suitable small rucksacks are available at most outdoor retailers. The photograph shows the sort of size and shape you might consider.

As well as shouldering your rope and rack a rucksack is also useful for carrying helmet, spare clothing, food, drink, and first-aid kit.

Clothing
There was a time when rock climbers went about their pursuit in uniformly drab tweeds of khaki, greys, and greens. These days, however, anything goes; sometimes everything – all at once. Visit a popular crag on a busy Saturday and you will be treated to a sartorial feast; the old guard, a few diehards excepted, have all but forsaken their tweeds for once-thought-to-be avant-garde tracksuit trousers and T-shirts; but anyone under thirty years of age and 80 kilograms (180 pounds) in weight is likely to be running a courting peacock a very close second. Indeed, the latest stretch-lycra creations might just be turning peacocks merely green – or whatever colour peacocks turn when they are envious. You can wear anything that is warm enough for the day – remember you might work very hard fighting your way up some off-width, and then spend half-an-

First-aid kit
It is always worth keeping a simple first-aid kit in your rucksack. You could take the following items, perhaps packed into a plastic lunch box:
roll of zinc oxide plaster;
crepe bandage;
plasters;
two triangular bandages;
two large wound dressings;
analgesic tablets;
insect repellent (especially where midges are known to be a problem;
knife (for a dozen things);
pencil and paper (for writing messages in the event of an accident);
suncream (optimists only).

Map and compass
These are hardly necessary on roadside crags but, for remote climbing areas, they are useful adjuncts to finding the way home when the sun has gone to mists. It is beyond the scope of this book to discuss navigation techniques; whole books have been written on the subject, some of which are mentioned in the Further Reading list.

CHAPTER 3

PROTECTING THE CLIMBS

There is a bewildering array of equipment available to today's climbers enabling them to undertake climbs more safely than the early pioneers. When people first began to climb rocks for sport and pleasure, there was very little in the way of protection devices for any of the climbers. Ropes were the only items of safety equipment used and, even those, because they were made of natural fibres, such as manila, hemp, and sisal, were of variable breaking strength and therefore not very reliable. Early climbers limited themselves to the more obvious lines on rock faces, such as easy gullies and ridges, but, as these features gradually became 'worked out', attention turned to the more tricky undertakings. Techniques were evolved for protecting the leader; these included untying from the rope, threading it through chockstones (stones wedged in a crack), and tying back on. As a refinement, climbers then began to carry short lengths of rope which could be threaded through and the ends tied together with the rope passing through the sling.

At the turn of the century and until the 1920s, many ascents were made in this style. The majority of climbs were quite easy by today's standards, but there are a few climbs which stand out as significant achievements and rank as highly respected undertakings even now. Problems were often overcome by the climbers standing on each other's shoulders. Although pitons were widely used in Europe, they were frowned upon by British climbers, to the extent that Geoffrey Winthrop Young, a pioneer of many a first ascent and a highly respected performer of his day once remarked that 'A man who would use pitons on British rock would shoot foxes'. Had these early climbers accepted the use of pitons, the style of British climbing might be very different today.

Karabiners and nylon ropes, available shortly before World War 2, did much to advance the standards of climbing although it is true to say that it was the personalities of the day that were the main protagonists of the rise in standards. When studying the history of rock climbing in Britain, for example, it is worth noting that a significant change took place after World War 2. Hitherto rock climbing and, indeed, mountaineering in general had been largely the preserves of the aristocracy – 'gentleman's sports'. After the war, things changed dramatically. It is difficult to pinpoint exactly why; perhaps people sought a release from the pressures of a war-torn world. Regardless of the reasons, climbing became a popular working man's sport. No-one epitomizes this change more than Joe Brown and the men of the Rock and Ice Climbing Club. They brought to the climbing scene a breath of fresh air and, more importantly, great skill in rock climbing and ideas for developing protection techniques and devices.

To begin with, small round pebbles were carried – rumour has it in the brim of their woolly hats! These pebbles would be inserted into a crack, a sling threaded around them, and the ends joined together with a karabiner. Pitons were used, albeit very judiciously, and only after careful consideration. Suddenly, with skill and great daring, almost anything was posible. 'Chockstoning', as it was known, was brought to a finer art by the idea of taking machined nuts, filing out the inside thread, and then threading them on to a sling which was then permanently knotted. These could then be inserted into cracks and the laborious and time-consuming task of threading them was avoided. It was natural that these ideas would be taken further and, eventually, climbers began to manufacture 'nuts' specifically for climbing. To begin with, these were designed along the same lines as the hexago-

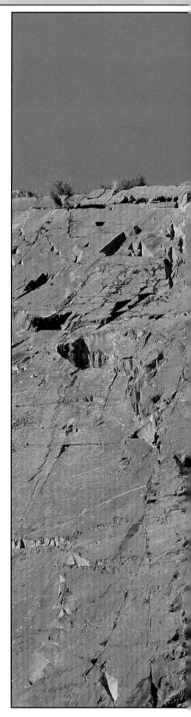

The leader of the climb must be careful to place protection to prevent a serious fall with perhaps fatal results.

nal machine nuts which had been used, but wedge-shaped nuts soon appeared and the MOAC, which was developed in the United Kingdom, is probably the most famous of this type. Still going strong today, it was first developed in the mid-'sixties.

From this point, rapid progress was made. Small-sized nuts were put on to wire slings because they were stronger than cord, and all sorts of shapes and sizes became available. A major breakthrough was achieved in the United States with the development by Yvon Chouinard of the **hexcentric nut.** This is a hexagonal nut which can be cammed into parallel-sided cracks. It is also worth noting that, in the 1960s, the traditional hawser-laid rope was superseded by stronger and easier-to-handle kernmantle rope, although the early types took time to be accepted.

There have been many developments, from plastic and rubber nuts to weird and wonderful shapes, which never caught on even though they all promised to take the climbing world by storm. Even today, inventions appear quite frequently only to die as quickly as they appeared. By far the most important development ever to take place was the invention of 'friends'. Largely the work of American climber, Ray Jardine, these devices have single-handedly revolutionized protection techniques, and have made previously bold and unprotected leads available to those with the skill to climb them even if they do not have the nerve to cope with the possibility of a lethal fall. That is not to say, there are no bold leads around, there are plenty. These devices can be placed in the most unusual cracks and crannies, and once you learn to trust them and to use them, they are indispensable items on a climber's gear rack. Many similar items have appeared, from 'buddies' to 'amigos' but none has surpassed the performance of the 'friend' and all the others seem destined for the junk heap.

In conclusion, the vast array of equipment available to today's rock climbers is quite confusing. Just about everything works to some

extent but, as in all things, some work better than others. Choosing equipment for a first time can be very confusing indeed but, in the remainder of this chapter, the pros and cons of the more commonly used items are considered so that you are left in little doubt about what is useful to have and what is not.

NUTS OR CHOCKS

These fall into two main categories: 'wedge' and 'hexcentric'. All items of protection come in sizes from 0 upwards, and some in half sizes. When referring to the size of nuts required for a climb, the majority of climbers refer to the trade name plus the number. Thus, one might

Above: A selection of wedge- and hexagonal-shaped chocks on rope.

Right: Here the leader is carrying chocks of varying shapes and sizes. Jerry Peel on the 'Dangler' an E3 5c climb in Borrowdale in the English Lake District.

hear a group of climbers discussing a route where the crux is protected by a 'brilliant Rock 7' (good, large runner in a solid placement – makes safe crux) or 'marginal R.P. 2' (very small nut in a placement that will probably come out if one fell on to it). Some people still refer to them as 'big ones' or 'small ones' but most

younger climbers today prefer to be more specific. As a general rule, it is safer to buy smaller nuts which have been prethreaded with wire slings. The wire sling is particularly strong and the joints are often stronger than the wire itself. Indeed, manufacturers should be commended for no longer selling loose nuts that take cord less than 6 millimetres (¼ inch) in diameter. Ideally, if you are buying nuts loose, you should be able to thread at least 8-millimetre (⅓-inch) cord through. This gives a minimum breaking strain of around 2000 kilograms (4400 pounds).

Wedge-shaped nuts

The traditional MOAC with straight sides has long since been superseded by more modern designs, although a MOAC is still a very useful addition to anyone's rack. By far the most commonly used wedges are those that have curved faces on them and, essentially, there are two main choices: The Wild Country 'Rock' and the Chouinard 'Stopper'. Both have curved faces with one convex side, the other concave. The Chouinard also has curved sides, one convex, one concave. A great deal of thought has gone into the design of these nuts, and they are much more versatile than straight wedge shapes. It is possible to place them securely in cracks that are almost parallel. Owing to the shape of the nut, a camming action can be achieved so that they are not only versatile in cracks but also in 'pockets' most commonly found on limestone. In practice, Wild Country Rocks perform marginally better than Chouinard Stoppers, particularly as they are easier to remove after use.

'R.P.s', designed by Australian climber Roland Pauligk, are usefully shaped nuts. Although they are straight sided, they are quite narrow and elongated wedges ('Foxheads' in the United States) making them suitable for shallow, wedge-shaped placement. The smallest size, 0, is very tiny indeed and, although the breaking strain of the wire is about 360 kilograms (800 pounds), the nut would probably pull out of the crack before the wire would break. This is a particular problem on 'softer'

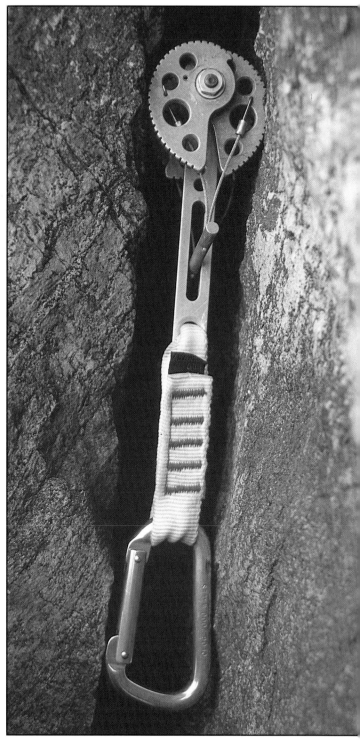

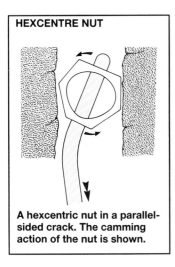

HEXCENTRE NUT

A hexcentric nut in a parallel-sided crack. The camming action of the nut is shown.

A well-placed friend. The development of these protection devices is one of the most important ever to take place in the climbing world.

rocks, such as limestone and sandstone. The biggest size, 5, is much less prone to this type of problem. The R.P. is a brass nut which is silver-soldered on to the wire so that there is no obvious joint; R.P.s are colour coded for ease of identification.

The most recent addition to the 'wedge family' is the 'Wallnut', manufactured by DMM International. 'Wallnuts' are versatile and perform most satisfactorily.

Hexcentrics

The very first commercially made nuts for climbers were designed along similar lines to the drilled-out engineering nuts, which, because they were hexagonal in shape, were ideally suited to placement in tapered cracks. It was soon discovered, however, that in use, the shape was no better than that of a wedge. Chouinard went on to develop something similar to the hexagonal nut, but discovered that, by making the five sides of unequal size, a camming action could be achieved and that it was possible to jam these 'hexcentric' shapes into parallel-sided cracks. It was a major breakthrough in protection.

Hexcentrics are available in sizes 1 through to 12. The size 12 is an enormous and unwieldy implement to carry. Certainly, a nut of that size should only be carried if it will definitely be required on the climb in a particular place. The smaller sizes are not so useful as the larger, except perhaps in situations where small pockets are encountered or in narrow horizontal cracks. For copyright reasons there are no other hexcentric nuts available although Clog did bring out a similar design some years ago called the 'Clog Cog', which for some reason did not become popular with climbers.

FRIENDS

There is no doubt that the development of friends has made the most significant technological contribution to the rise in climbing standards over recent years. Their versatility, ease of placement, and ability to provide protection in previously impossible situations have made them popular, not only with top climbers, but across the whole spectrum of performance levels. Work first began on this device in the early 1970s by American climber, Ray Jardine, and they went into commercial production in 1977. Since that time, the design has remained the same but the technology has improved to the extent that they are now much smaller, lighter and stronger.

A friend consists of four independently operating cams. Each cam works in a way that mathematicians call *the constant-angle curve or logarithmic spiral*. This 'constant-angle cam' means that the cam is in contact with the rock surface at the same angle, regardless of its placement and, with two cams on each side of the camshaft, when a load is exerted, the friend bites deeper into the placement. Each cam operates independently, enabling it to grip in irregularly shaped cracks. Owing to the action of the constant-angle cams, friends can be placed in inverted tapered cracks (*see illustration*) and are able to cope with flared cracks with angles of up to 30 degrees.

Friends come in sizes from 1 through to 4 including half sizes. There is now a range of Technical Friends from 0 to 1½ including half sizes. These recent developments are much more compact than traditional friends and have a flexible wire stem rather than a rigid one. Each comes with a colour-coded sewn sling attached, although it is possible to remove this and replace it with another sling of your own choice. Not many climbers take this option but, if for some reason you choose to do so, you can see how it should be threaded.

Because they are such complex devices, friends are not without their problems which, although these are few, they usually arise from the inability of the climber to use them correctly. The following points should be borne in mind when placing friends:

1. Do not place the friend too deep in the crack. The cam release trigger may be very difficult to get to for extraction.

2. Always re-align the friend if one or more of the cams does not bite into the crack walls.

3. Do not allow the cams to become inverted. The friend loses all its holding power.

4. Avoid placements where the cams are open too wide. Friends placed with the tips of the cams just touching the sides are unable to expand further and lose holding power. Remove the friend and use the next size up.

5. Do not 'cram the cams'. Forcing the friend into too tight a placement makes it difficult to extract. Use the next size down.

6. For optimum performance, the size of the friend should be such that the cam release trigger is in the middle third of its total length of travel in the retaining slot.

7. Always close the cams completely before placement and allow them to open inside the crack. Never force the friend into a crack hoping it will grip.

8. Ensure that the friend is well slung to minimize movement after placement.

Above all else, friends must be placed confidently. They grip remarkably well even in surprisingly

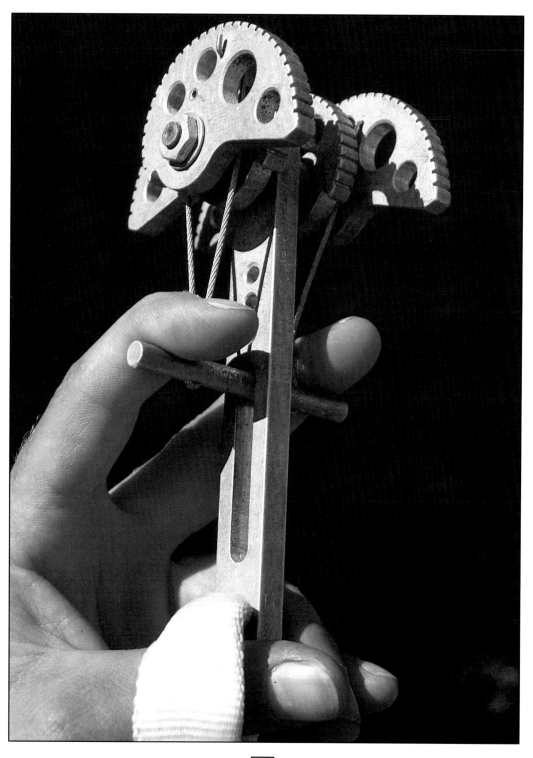

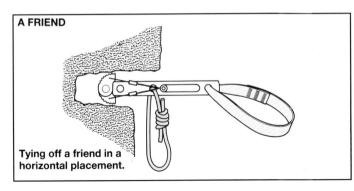
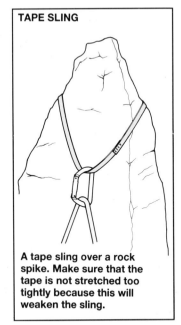

TAPE SLING

A tape sling over a rock spike. Make sure that the tape is not stretched too tightly because this will weaken the sling.

poor placements, so experiment with them in 'safe' situations. Put heavy loads on them and see how they perform. Take care about using friends in horizontal placements, especially where the stem sticks out a long way and a fall would result in an enormous amount of leverage being placed on the stem. If a friend is used in a horizontal placement, the leverage problem can be overcome by threading 4-millimetre cord through the 'tie-off' hole between the cams and the release trigger. Obviously, this has to be done before use. A second sling on the friend can be a hindrance at times because it may get in the way of operation, so think carefully before doing it because it may not be necessary until you are more familiar with climbing and gear.

Extraction of friends is sometimes difficult and poses more problems than any other single factor. Often, it results from poor placement, an inevitable occurrence from time to time. Sometimes, it may be difficult to remove a friend with one hand while you are hanging on with the other. In that case, hang on the rope to allow both hands to be used. It may even be necessary to use a special extractor although this is an extra item of kit to carry and usually not necessary. Wild Country makes a nut key which has two hooks on one end which are specifically designed for friend removal. A nut key is a more-or-less essential piece of kit so that it is well worth getting

one with the extraction hooks when you buy this item of kit.

Because a friend has so many moving parts, it is necessary to keep them clean and well lubricated. A silicone-based lubricant is best. Ordinary oils will make friends very unpleasant to handle. Make sure any excess lubricant is removed. Occasionally, things go wrong with them. Do not try to repair them yourself. Wild Country offers an excellent repair service at reasonable cost.

OTHER TECHNOLOGY

The items of equipment already mentioned are by far the most commonly used throughout the world, so they have been described in some detail. There are, however, many more protection devices available. Some of the items of equipment mentioned below may be useful.

HB offset nuts
These are small wedge-shaped brass nuts with a transverse asymmetric taper, suitable for use in shallow, rounded cracks and pockets.

Tricams
Tricams are interesting and worth considering although larger sizes are unwieldy and heavy. They work exceptionally well in deep pockets, but they may be tricky to place with one hand. They can work loose and fall out.

Roller nuts
These are adjustable wedge-shaped nuts. They are expensive and awkward to place.

'Buddies', 'Amigos', and 'Bivos'
All these are essentially similar to the friend but, if popular usage is anything to go by, they are much less effective.

Slings
There is nothing very technological about slings but they are essential. They are used for draping over spikes of rock, around trees, or for threading through chockstones. A variety of lengths are available. Nowadays, most climbers carry tape slings. Some still prefer rope slings. Tape is a more versatile material for slings, however, because it is easier to handle and can fit in more places than the roped variety. It is possible to make up your own slings by buying tape (or rope) from a roll, cutting it to the required length, and joining it with a 'tape knot' or double fisherman's knot in the case of rope. Ready made-up slings with stitched joints are commonly available in two sizes: 1.2-metre (4-foot) and 2.4-metre (8-foot). Ready-made slings cannot come undone and they are much more compact in use. Occasionally, tape knots can work loose and any

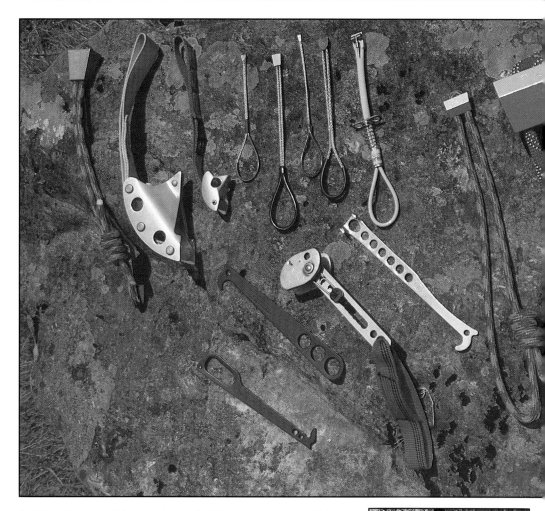

knotted slings must be checked regularly.

Tape slings are also available as 'quick draws' or 'extensions'. These items of kit are used for extending running belays to reduce rope drag and to prevent wire placements from falling out. DMM Equipment manufactures a 'shock tape' sling which is sewn in a concertina style. The strength of the stitching is such that it is supposed to break open gradually if a climber falls on it. This reduces the ultimate strain on the running belay and is ideal for marginal placements, and for the system as a whole.

Tape is available in two types: flat and tubular. The flat variety tends to be harder wearing but it is not so flexible as tubular tape. It is also available in a variety of widths: 2.5 and 1.5 centimetre (1 inch and ⅗ inch) are the most common.

CARRY EQUIPMENT OR RACKING

Many climbers, even experienced ones, pay little attention to the way in which all the equipment is carried. So often people on crags have to fumble for gear because they do not know where it is on the harness or bandolier; this wastes valuable strength and time. It is well worth investing some time, thought, and preparation into your rack. After all, it is an essential part of the overall

Above: An assortment of protection equipment. From left to right. Top row: A MOAC, two tri-cams, an HB offset, two RPs, a Wild Country micronut, and a rollernut. Bottom row: two nut keys, an Edelrid bivo, nut key with friend extraction hooks, and two hexcentrics.

Left: A sling placed through a 'thread' and the ends clipped together with a karabiner. Make sure that the edges of the crack do not have any sharp edges.

Right: Carrying equipment on a bandolier. Not all the equipment is on the bandolier but the components are separated.

Left: Carrying the equipment on the harness gear loops. The method of carrying equipment is largely a matter of personal preference. Experiment with different systems.

Above: A perfectly placed 'Rock' 9, one of the two main choices of wedge-shaped nuts.

safety chain, and you will undoubtedly find that being well organized with your gear makes climbing that little bit more pleasurable and rewarding. Unfortunately, as we have already seen, there is a vast array of protection equipment available, and it is not easy to choose a suitable rack. On page 48 are described two basic racks of gear which are suitable for beginning rock climbing – one is for the thrifty and one for the affluent. Once you have bought the kit, you then must decide how it is to be carried. There are two ways: on a bandolier; or on the harness gear racks.

Bandoliers have the main advantage that the gear is contained in one place, and, if they are leading through on routes, climbers simply swap bandoliers. The main disadvantages are that they make you feel rather lopsided and that, if you are climbing slabs or easy-angled rock, the bandolier tends to swing around in front of you and obscures the view of your feet.

The gear racks on harnesses are quite good nowadays, and some manufacturers offer the facility to choose where you want to put gear racks. There are a few disadvantages in carrying equipment this way. Firstly, if you have a lot of heavy equipment, it tends to drag the waist belt down around the hips making long days in the harness uncomfortable. Secondly, if you are carrying any big nuts on long rope slings, they tend to dangle around your knees and cause bruising!

If you can, you should experiment with both systems. Whichever system you use, there should be some order about the way in which it is racked. The two photographs show the two systems described. Note particularly that: **1.** nuts, friends, and so on are racked according to size, with the smallest ones at the front; **2.** all karabiners face the same way and are of similar size and make; **3.** quick draws and spare krabs are easily accessible; **4.** gear that is not needed while leading is well out of the way; **5.** slings are all carried in the same bandolier fashion, and long ones are draped around with the ends clipped together. This enables the climber to remove long slings without lifting them over the head and having to take both hands off the rock. Wired nuts are grouped by size and carried on one karabiner. This has the advantage that, if you see a crack that you think might take a particular size nut, but then you find it does not, at least you have similar sizes to try out without having to get another set off the rack. This system has a very major drawback which you will soon discover when you drop the karabiner containing a few nuts.

PLACING PROTECTION

To begin with, you will find it difficult to select the right piece of protection to use in a particular crack. It is well worth experimenting with the gear first in a controlled situation. One of the most difficult techniques is to 'see' placements. Some, such as well-tapered cracks, are obvious. You should always try to get the largest possible nut in the crack. This gives maximum jamming advantage. The photograph shows an excellent placement for a Rock 9. Note the acute taper of the crack. Less acutely tapered cracks may still give good placements but it will be necessary to exert a bit of pressure on the nut to ensure it is seated in the crack firmly. Often, you will find that it will be necessary to hang on with one hand while you place protection. Try to get as comfortable as possible and take most of the weight on your feet. If your arm gets tired you can always juggle your position and swap hands for a bit of a rest.

Wired runners

Once you have placed a wire runner in a crack, you must remove the karabiner with the remaining wires on it and clip in an extension of some kind. Clipping in a karabiner is acceptable on steep walls when the placement is good but, invariably, wires need to be extended with either two karabiners or a quick draw. Never loop a tape directly through the wire because the diameter of the wire is too small and, in the event of a fall, will work like a knife on the tape. Always extend either with two karabiners or a krab/sling/krab. The reason for having to extend wire runners is that, when the rope runs through them, it creates a lot of leverage on the nut placement. This happens because the wire is so stiff. Extending it to create a hinge effect, reduces the possibility of the nut falling out accidentally. This problem does not occur so much with rope-slung nuts because the sling is flexible enough to reduce the leverage on the nut.

From time to time, you will have to consider extending any type of running belay for reasons such as those below.

1. The next moves of the climb require the climber to move around an overlap or overhang. Clipping the climbing rope into the runner directly causes excessive rope drag.

2. A runner may be off to one side of

the route to be taken, and clipping in directly causes the rope to run through a sharp bend. This will give considerable rope drag particularly if you are using a single rope.

Roped nuts

If you buy nuts loose, you will also need to buy some rope or tape on which to thread the nut. The length of sling used is quite critical in that, if it is too long, it will be an awkward and cumbersome item to carry and, if it is too short, you will need to extend it each time it is used. The more runners that require extensions you have, the more quick draws you will need to carry. Also of critical importance is the thickness of cord that you buy. It is not advisable to get the thickest cord and cram it through. Doing this will actually weaken the cord considerably. The cord should be of a diameter that will slide easily through the holes of the nut with a very small amount of friction. You should bear in mind that cord less than 8 millimetres in diameter has a much lower breaking strength than the rest of the safety chain. For this reason, you would be well advised to limit the number of small roped nuts carried, in favour of wired ones. As a rough guide 1.25 metres (4 feet) of cord will give a suitable length sling by the time the ends are tied with a double fisherman's knot. Always tighten the knot as much as possible before use and keep a constant check on it. Make sure that there is at least 4 centimetres (1½ inches) of ends sticking out of the knot. It may be worth considering using tape instead of cord, but remember that the tape is more prone to working loose. On large hexcentrics, it is possible to tie the knot inside the nut.

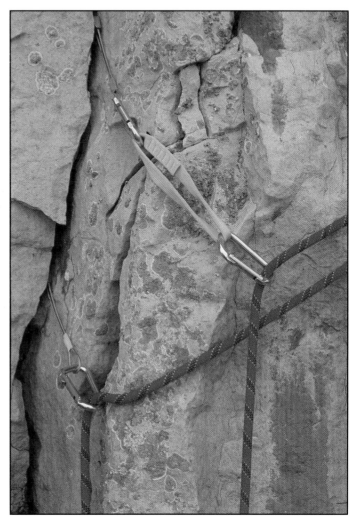

Above: Extending wire runners reduces leverage, friction and rope drag.

Right: The second approaching a running belay. The runner has been extended using a karabiner, a sling, then a krab. The climb is the 'Girdle Traverse' of Dinas Gromlech in North Wales.

A LOW-COST RACK		Something a little more expensive!
2 × large stitched slings (2.4 m × 25 mm)	1 × Rock 3 on wire	As above but add;
2×screwgate karabiners for the above	1 × Rock 5 on wire	1 × Friend 2
	1 × Rock 6 on wire	1 × Friend 3
2 × small stitched slings (1.2 m × 25 mm)	1 × Rock 7 on wire	1 × Rock 1, 2, 4, and 8
	1 × Rock 9 on wire	2 × quick draws
2 × snaplink karabiners for the above	1 × hexcentric 6 on rope	1 × R.P. 3, 4, and 5
	1 × hexcentric 9 on rope	10 × lightweight karabiners
	4 × quick draws	
	12 × snaplink karabiners	

CHAPTER 4

ROPEWORK

Ropes are used for the general safety of the climbing party. Ropework is probably the most complicated aspect of rock climbing, but do not be put off if you fail to grasp everything from the beginning. There are hundreds of climbers who still have not mastered it even after years of experience, and some of them are quite well known. It is important that you evolve a system of some kind. Initially, this need only be very simple, but it should be one that can be added to and improved upon as you progress and become more proficient in general rope handling. There are many systems that could be used, and you will doubtless see all sorts in your experience but it is imperative that you do not sacrifice safety for simplicity in any way. The first part of this chapter describes a system of ropework that is perfectly satisfactory and which is about as simple a system as can be devised while still retaining the elements of versatility and adaptability. Practise the individual elements of ropework described before 'putting it all together'. Later on, we will discuss the more advanced and problematical situations you may find yourself in.

KNOTS

There are many different kinds of knots that could be used in the rock climbing safety chain. Fortunately, it is possible to get by with very few knots. Knots should be practised thoroughly before you go out into the 'real world'. As a general guide to competence, you should be able to tie all the knots required with your eyes closed. If you have the slightest doubt about whether a knot is tied correctly, you should untie it and start again. Remember that practice makes perfect.

The figure of eight knot
This is probably the most useful knot a climber can learn. It has many uses and can be tied in a number of different ways. The end result is always the same; the variable is what you need to tie it into. The

double loop that is formed in the first instance is called a 'bight' and it should be about 50 centimetres (20 inches) long (slightly less with 9-millimetre rope). This will ensure that there is enough tail end of rope sticking out once the knot has been tied. It is important to finish the knot off with a **stopper** knot because the knot is then unlikely to come undone during use. Now is a good time to learn this knot well because, each time you tie a knot in the end of the rope, it should be finished off with a stopper knot.

One of the good things about the figure eight knot is that, as long as you do not miss out a strand of rope when tying it, it is still quite safe. If you do not do enough turns, the result is an **overhand** knot – quite safe but difficult to undo after a heavy load has been applied to it. If

you do too many turns, the result is a figure of sixteen or even a figure of thirty-two!

To use the figure eight knot to tie the rope to the harness, it is necessary to tie the knot in the single rope about 75 centimetres (30 inches) from the end of the rope. Thread the end through the **tie-on** loops of the harness according to the manufacturer's recommendations, and then thread the end back through the knot until you have traced all the loops. Remember to finish it off with the stopper knot for safety. This is always most important.

To begin with, these two methods of tying the knot are sufficient for your needs.

At this stage it is well worth mentioning the **central loop** because it will be referred to constantly throughout the text.

FIGURE EIGHT KNOT

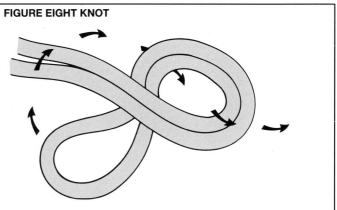

Tying a figure of eight knot in a bight of the rope.

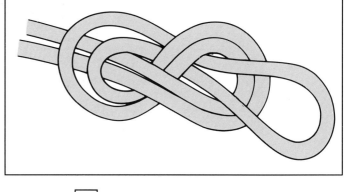

If you look closely at the illustration you will see that when the figure eight is completed, as an attachment of the rope to the harness a loop should not be very big. As a guide to size, you should not be able to put your hand through it. This loop is a very strong attachment point and plays an integral part in the belay system described. For ease of identification it can be called the **central loop**.

Clove hitch

The clove hitch is the second of the knots required for the system of ropework that is described in this chapter. It is a wonderful knot, not least because of its simplicity, but also because it can be so easily adjusted. It is very important that you learn to tie it correctly. Tied incorrectly, it is a very dangerous knot to use in the belaying system described.

As with all knots, once it is learned, it is often possible to evolve a personal method of tying; as long as the finished product is correct it does not really matter how it is tied. Once you have clipped the knot into a karabiner, it can be easily adjusted by feeding either of the ropes through until the desired tension is required. Under normal useage, the clove hitch does not become tight and difficult to undo, but, if a severe load is placed on it, it can be quite a problem.

TYING ON TO ANCHOR POINTS

In Chapter 3 the different types of rock fixings available are considered. Some require much practice at placing them before you can be sure that they are secure enough to hold you and your partner in an emergency. Quite often, there will be very solid and obvious anchor points available, particularly on the easier climbs that you will be learning on. Once you embark on your climb, you will need to secure yourself to the rock at intervals. These intervals are referred to as **stances**, and they occur at the end of a pitch (dealt with in more detail in the next section).

It is very important to take note of two significant matters when tying on to anchors. Firstly, you must ensure that you are held tightly on the anchor. This does not necessarily mean that you should be hanging your full body weight off it but that, in the event of your partner falling off, you will not be pulled violently forward before the anchor holds you. This could put extra strain on the anchors, and the shock-loading could be enough to pull the anchors out or, more likely, to pull you off balance causing you to let go of the belay plate. Similarly, the direction of pull should be anticipated if your partner falls off. You must ensure that the rope from the anchor runs in a straight line from the anchor through you and on down to your partner in the anticipated direction of pull. If there is an angle in the

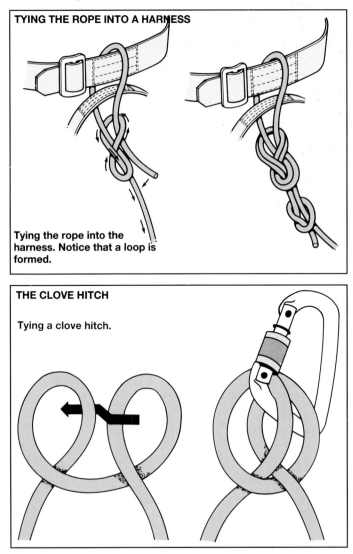

TYING THE ROPE INTO A HARNESS

Tying the rope into the harness. Notice that a loop is formed.

THE CLOVE HITCH

Tying a clove hitch.

system, you will certainly be pulled to one side, the severity of which depends on the size of the angle. This could also cause you to let go of your partner's rope. A combination of these two factors often leads to drastic consequences so you would be well advised to pay close attention to them during the climb.

Tying on to a single anchor

There is a number of different methods of securing oneself to an anchor point but, to simplify matters, there is a straightforward, safe system that is easy to learn and to remember. This system requires two screwgate karabiners, one of which should be a large pear-shaped krab. The other should be of reasonable size but need not necessarily be a pear shape.

Having placed your anchor point, clip the pear-shaped krab into the central loop and the second screwgate into the anchor. Clip the rope through the anchor krab and **screw up the gate**. Move into the position you are going to belay from. Always try to sit down because it is

generally more stable and therefore easier to hold a fall from a sitting position. Take up the slack climbing rope and tie a clove hitch; this is then clipped into the pear-shaped krab and the gate screwed up. Now all you need to do is to adjust the knot until the rope between yourself and the anchor point is tight. For safety reasons, you should use a screwgate karabiner for the clove hitch but, if you do not have one for the anchor point, two snaplinks can be used. All you need do for safety is to arrange them so that the gates open on opposite sides. This prevents the rope becoming unclipped accidentally.

This, then, is the basic system. But occasionally, it is possible to clip yourself into the anchor directly without having to use the rope. If this is the case, make sure that the length of sling that you use coincides with where you have to sit or

'Maxines Wall', a 5:10 climb in Yosemite Valley, California, United States. The second is anchored to the cliff and is belaying the leader who places running belays.

stand on the stance so that you can be tight on to the anchor. Because of the simplicity of this method, you should never discount it when rigging a stance.

The belay plate

In days gone by, a climber's rope was safeguarded by the partner holding the rope around the body. The friction generated in doing this enabled much better grip on the rope in the event of a fall. Many climbers still use a system such as the **waist belay** and, much less commonly, the **shoulder belay**. While these methods are safe for the

SINGLE ANCHOR POINT

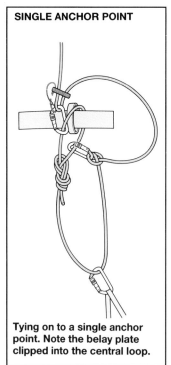

Tying on to a single anchor point. Note the belay plate clipped into the central loop.

THE SNAPLINKS

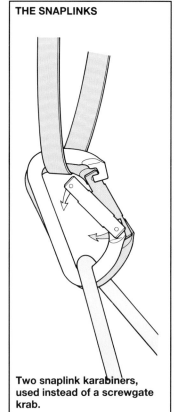

Two snaplink karabiners, used instead of a screwgate krab.

FIGURE EIGHT KNOT

An alternative way of tying on to an anchor point is to use a figure of eight knot This is tied through the central loop, making sure that there is at least 30 centimetres (12 inches) of spare tail.

expert, in unpractised hands they can be lethal. As a beginner to the sport, it is sensible and safer to use a special device called a **belay plate**. (*See* Chapter 2.) The use of the waist belay is discussed on page 65.

Many people think that a belay plate is an automatic locking device but this is not true. While it certainly makes holding the rope with a weight on the end a lot easier, care is still needed in using it.

As mentioned in Chapter 2, there are many types available. One without a spring and capable of taking both 9-millimetre and 11-millimetre ropes is probably the most useful to have though, at the beginner's stage, you will be using one rope only. As you become more experienced, you may discover the need for two (*see* double rope technique on page 58). You will also need a screwgate karabiner and a short piece of 4-millimetre (0.15-inch) cord to complete the belaying ensemble. The cord is required to prevent the belay plate from sliding away down the rope during use. The karabiner could be any screwgate but a pear-shaped or HMS is perfect for the job. The most important thing to consider is that the karabiner must not have acute (tight) bends in it because they would cause the rope to 'grab' and make handling the rope much more awkward than it need be if there were no such bends.

When using the belay plate, it is important to ensure that you have enough room to **lock off** if you need to hold a climber's weight. The photograph shows a climber holding the rope in the locked-off position. Note that there is ample room to bring the **controlling hand** back effectively to **lock off** the plate. During use, the controlling hand plays a very important role. Put bluntly, if you let go of the controlling rope while holding a climber, that person will fall to the ground. It is of paramount importance, therefore, that you keep a firm grip on the rope at all times to hold even a surprise fall. These things do happen. *See* the sequence of photographs showing the operation of the belay plate.

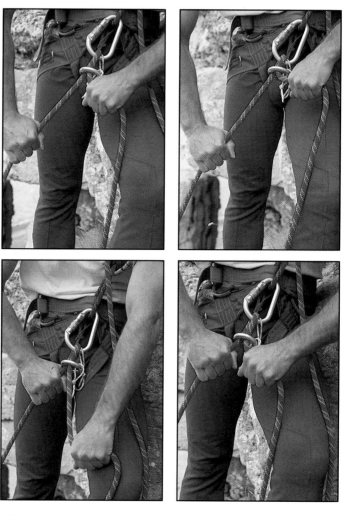

Taking in and **paying out** the rope require a lot of practice, so choose somewhere safe to begin with. Success is largely a matter of dexterity and the ability to remain calm during the early stages of learning. Occasionally, the rope may jam in the belay plate. This is to be expected and will happen from time to time no matter how experienced you become. As a tip to ease of handling, remember never to let go of the controlling rope – the hand that holds that rope should only be allowed to slide along the rope; it must never let go completely. If you need to manipulate the rope in any other way, use the hand that controls the **live rope**.

Top left to bottom right: Taking in the rope through a belay plate. The 'live' rope is in the belayer's right hand and the left is the 'controlling' hand. Never let go of the controlling rope.

Initially, it will be quite tricky to keep the rope in a neat pile at your feet but, as you become more familiar with the equipment, try to keep it as neatly as possible and do not allow it to fall down the face where it may become tangled.

Tying off a belay plate
This is a most useful technique to learn because it can be used tempo-

rarily to secure your partner on changeovers at stances or at any time during the climb when you may want to use two hands to do something.

PUTTING IT ALL TOGETHER

Once you have mastered the rudiments of ropework, you are ready to set out on a climb. Broadly speaking, rock climbs fall into two main categories: **single-pitch climbs** and **multi-pitch climbs**.

Each category can be tackled in different ways. Single-pitch climbs can be done either by going to the top of the cliff and dropping a rope down to the person who is going to do the climb. Or they can be done by arranging the rope around an anchor point at the top and using this as a pulley system so that the climber can be safeguarded from below. Both these techniques are referred to as **top roping**. A third way of tackling a one-pitch climb is for one person to lead the climb, fix an anchor at the top, and bring the next climber up to the top.

Both climbers begin on the ground where they uncoil their ropes into a neat pile and tie themselves on. The **leader** is the climber who ascends the cliff first. Obviously, this person is in the most dangerous position because he/she does not have rope protection from above. The leader can protect himself or herself to a certain extent by the judicious use of **running belays** (described in Chapter 3). The **second** puts the leader's rope through a belay plate to hold the leader should he/she fall off. It does sound a rather terrifying possibility that the leader might fall but it is not an unknown occurrence. There used to be a saying that the leader should never fall. Certainly in the 1930s and even the 1960s that was a good policy to follow because there was little in the way of sophisticated equipment for the leader to place to

Tying off a belay plate. This can be quite tricky to do with someone hanging on the end of the rope so make sure that you practise it.

TOP ROPING

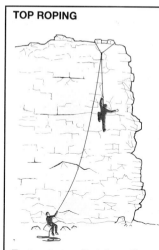

Top roping a climb from the ground. Make sure that the rope at the anchor point runs through a screwgate krab.

give some protection. It is quite different today, however, and, with the variety of gear available to suit so many different situations, there is little excuse for a falling leader to go very far but that is not to say that every rock climb is now safe. The worst cases of leader falls are often as a result of a sloppy belaying by the second, so make sure you climb with someone who is as concerned about your life as you are yourself!

If the leader should fall, the second will experience an **upward pull** on the rope. In most cases, it will be possible for the second to hold the rope quite easily. If there is a large weight or force involved, however, the second may well be lifted off the ground. To avoid this possibility, an **upward pulling anchor** should be set up. This is an anchor point that will stop the second from being pulled upwards if the leader falls. It must be said,

however, that it is not always possible or convenient to do this, and much has to be left to the individual to decide how important a factor it is in each situation.

Anyway, back to the climb. The leader should climb up to a convenient ledge or stopping place on the cliff. This need not be a full rope's length from the second – indeed, it is rarely so. Neither should it be only 3 metres (10 feet) above the second for such short stages would make the climb seem very tedious. This part of a climb is called a **pitch**. Each pitch is referred to in the order it appears on the climb. The leader must now select anchor points and then secure himself/herself to them. Until this is done, the second must not take the rope out of the belay plate. The sequence of climbing calls shown on page 58 gives an indication of when to do what with the rope during the climb.

THE SEQUENCE OF MOVEMENT UP THE CLIFF

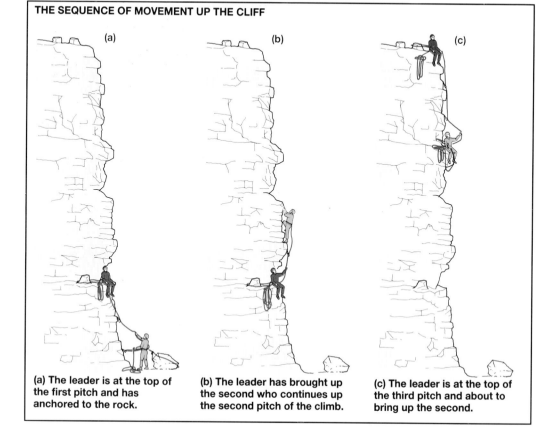

(a) The leader is at the top of the first pitch and has anchored to the rock.

(b) The leader has brought up the second who continues up the second pitch of the climb.

(c) The leader is at the top of the third pitch and about to bring up the second.

Once the leader is secured and the second has taken the rope out of the belay plate, all the slack rope between the two climbers must be taken up. This is done by the leader and is placed in a neat pile on the ledge. The second now prepares to climb while the leader places his/her rope in the belay plate. On an agreed signal, the second begins to climb and, as he/she does so, takes out any running belays the leader may have placed. On arrival at the **stance** the second could become the leader. This is known as **leading through** and is very much quicker than changing over on the stance at the end of each pitch. It does, of course, assume that both climbers are of equal competence not only to climb, but also to rig the anchors, and so on. If the leading-through technique is adopted, the person who seconded the previous pitch collects any gear that the other per-

son may have left on the rack, and carries straight on through to the top of the next pitch. This procedure is repeated all the way to the end of the climb.

If there is only one person capable of leading, the changeover at the end of each pitch should be effected as smoothly and as safely as possible. On arrival at the stance, the second must first tie into the anchor or anchor points before the leader takes the rope out of the belay plate. Once this is done, the rope must be reversed so that the end attached to the leader is on the top of the pile. The equipment must also be sorted out again and racked. Before the leader unties from the anchors, the second must have put the rope in the belay plate. In doing this, each of the climbers remains safe throughout the changeover.

It all sounds rather straightforward on paper and really it is. Inevit-

ably, though, things will get in a bit of a tangle from time to time, particularly if the stance is quite tiny. Stay calm though and it will be less agonizing as you gain more experience.

Tying on to more than one anchor point

There will inevitably be occasions when it is necessary to tie on to more than one anchor point. There may be many reasons for this, not least that one anchor point might not be considered to be strong enough to take the strain in an emergency, but two together combine to give a sound, secure anchor. When tying into multiple anchors, the criteria mentioned earlier are particularly important. To recap, these are:
1. being tight to the anchor point; and **2.** having the rope to the anchor in a straight line along the direction of anticipated fall. When using multiple anchors, a third important factor is introduced. To put it as simply as possible, you should use a system of tying-in so that, if one anchor point fails completely, the second or back-up anchor must take the strain without being subjected to a shock-loading.

The basic system of tying on to anchors described in the early part of this chapter is ideally suited to tying on to multiple anchors. Suppose that you find yourself in a situation where a second anchor point is necessary. Tie into the first one as usual and then *either:*
1. Take the rope from the clove hitch, which is tied into the central loop, up to the second anchor through a karabiner, and clove hitch it back into the same karabiner as the first clove hitch. Adjust the knot until the ropes to both anchors take equal strain. Remember to screw up the karabiner! *or:*
2. If the second anchor is within arm's reach of your stance, simply clip a clove hitch directly into a karabiner in that anchor. Adjust the knot to get the desired equal tension. A word of warning here – if the anchor is out of arm's reach, it is very difficult and impractical to adjust the clove hitch correctly; therefore, the first option must be employed. You will never have any problems if you

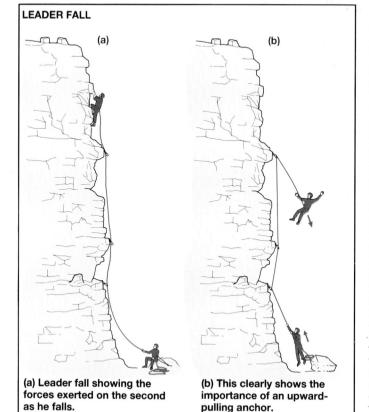

LEADER FALL

(a)

(b)

(a) Leader fall showing the forces exerted on the second as he falls.

(b) This clearly shows the importance of an upward-pulling anchor.

follow this simple rule throughout all your climbing days.

A third option is worthy of consideration. If the anchor points are close together, they can be linked together with a long sling. Clip the sling into both anchors and then tie an overhand knot in the doubled tape. This forms a single point of attachment, but to two anchor points, and may come in useful in situations where there is not enough rope to go back and fourth to two anchors. It is essential to tie a knot in the sling, otherwise, if one anchor fails, there will be a catastrophic failure of the whole system. Alternatively, you could put a clove hitch at each of the points where there is a karabiner. Remember to use a screwgate or double snaplink at the point where you clip in the rope.

Climbing calls and actions

LEADER	SECOND
'SAFE' or 'ON BELAY' Only shouted when leader is anchored to the rock face on a stance *or* is on safe ground where a fall is not possible.	Takes rope out of belay plate.
'TAKING IN' Takes in the slack rope between the two climbers.	Makes sure that the rope runs smoothly without knots or tangles.
On hearing this call the leader puts the rope into as belay device.	**'THAT'S ME'** When the rope comes tight. Must not undo from the anchor yet.
'CLIMB WHEN READY' Leader has rope in belay device before shouting this.	Now undoes the belay knots and remove anchors.
Leader is now responsible for the safety of the second as he/she is no longer secured to the mountainside.	**'CLIMBING'** Shouts this as soon as the anchors are undone. Final check to see nothing has been left behind.
'OK'	
'WATCH ME' Leader having difficulties and thinks he might fall off.	**'TIGHT ROPE'** Having similar difficulties to the leader.
'GOT ME? GOT ME?' Leader about to fall off.	**'TAKE IN'** Some slack has developed and is making the second nervous or it is in the way.
'SLACK' Requires second to pay out the rope.	**'SLACK'** Requires leader to pay out the rope.
'WHAT DOES THE GUIDEBOOK SAY?' Leader finding it a bit difficult and can not believe that the climb really goes up there.	**'WHERE DID YOU GO HERE'** Similar problem!

Double rope technique

When you first begin to climb, you will almost certainly climb on a single 11-millimetre rope. This is more than adequate for easier climbs and is much simpler to begin with. As you progress, however, and you want to tackle harder and more complicated climbs, it will be necessary to climb using two ropes. The illustrations show clearly the advantage of double-rope technique. It is obvious that using a single rope in this situation would have given an intolerable amount of rope drag. Indeed, the climber may not have been able to have so many running belays for protection, using a single rope. Nine-millimetre ropes are usually used for double-rope technique. Buy two separate 45-metre (150-foot) lengths. It is also sensible to make sure they are different

---

USING THE ANCHOR POINTS

Another method of bringing two anchor points together with a sling.

Tying on to more than one anchor point. The climber has tied on to the main anchor as described and has clipped into the second one with a clove hitch. Notice that the climber is tight on to the anchor points, has equal tension on both, and is in line with the anticipated direction of pull.

colours. Occasionally, climbers use a combination of thicknesses, 9 and 11 millimetre, 8.8 and 10 millimetre, or even two 11-millimetre ropes. The latter are very heavy to manipulate, particularly after a long pitch, and increased rope drag may make climbing more difficult.

Problems arise quite often when using two ropes, due largely to poor rope management. Before setting

USING TWO ANCHOR POINTS

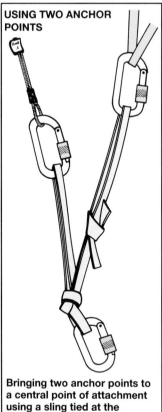

Bringing two anchor points to a central point of attachment using a sling tied at the attachment point with an overhand knot.

MULTIPLE ANCHOR POINTS

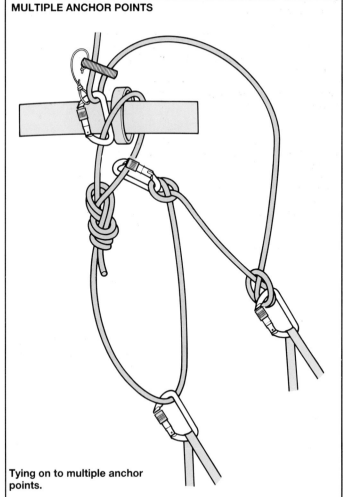

Tying on to multiple anchor points.

Poor use of double rope technique! The climber has got the ropes crossed and may well experience problems later on the pitch. Careful thought could avoid this problem.

---

out on a pitch, try to get some idea of where and how you will use each rope. In its simplest form, this means clipping one rope into runners on your left and one rope to your right. Try also to clip alternate ropes into alternate runners. Inevitably, though, you will end up clipping more runners on one than the other. The illustration shows a few good reasons why this may be the case. You can see quite clearly that a fall would result in only one rope taking the strain. As this may only be 9 millimetres thick, it is equivalent to climbing on a single 9-millimetre rope, and this is not to be recommended. Because of the friction generated by the rope passing through runners and the belay device, however, and the shock absorption properties of rope, harness, and bodies, it is rarely possible to generate enough strain to cause the rope to break (*see* **fall factor** page 64).

Other irritating problems, such as crossing the ropes, can more easily be avoided by thinking carefully before and during the climb. When using double ropes, you will of course need a belay plate with two slots. Both ropes can be clipped into the same krab – preferably a

DOUBLE ROPE TECHNIQUE

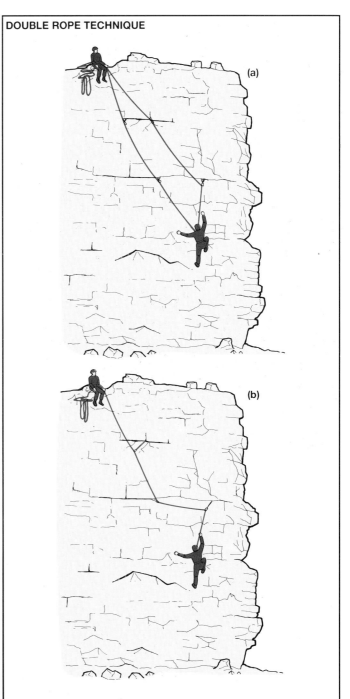

(a)

(b)

An advantage of using two ropes: leader (a) has placed the same number of running belays as leader (b), but is clearly burdened with much less rope drag.

large pear-shaped one. Tying on to multiple anchors is rather more straightforward because you can clip one rope into each anchor.

OTHER KNOTS

The figure of eight knot and the clove hitch are the two main knots used in the ropework system. There are, however, other knots that you will need to use from time to time. These knots are illustrated below and their main uses listed.

TAPE KNOT

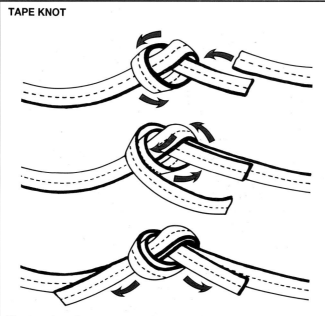

The tape knot is used to join the ends of a tape sling.

DOUBLE FISHERMAN'S KNOT

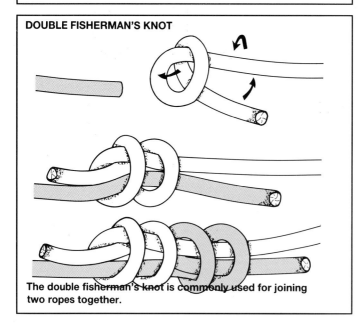

The double fisherman's knot is commonly used for joining two ropes together.

ITALIAN HITCH

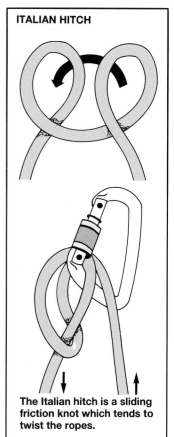

The Italian hitch is a sliding friction knot which tends to twist the ropes.

Double fisherman's knot

This is the most commonly used knot for joining rope ends together. It is used on rope slings for chocks and for joining two ropes together for abseiling. It is quite easy to tie incorrectly but it is obvious if it has been tied wrongly.

Italian hitch

This is a sliding friction knot which can be used as a belaying knot or abseil 'device'. It has a tendency to twist the ropes badly, although this can be overcome to a certain extent by using a large, pear-shaped kara-biner. If you are using it with double ropes, it will be easier to handle if you tie one knot with both ropes. Some texts recommend that you should tie a clove hitch in each rope and clip into separate karabiners but this only serves to twist the slack ropes together very badly.

Tape knot

This is used to join the ends of a tape sling. It can also be used on rope. Ensure that the tape lies flat and without twists throughout the knot and has at least 5 centimetres (2 inches) tail end after tying. The tape knot is prone to working loose, so keep a check on it.

Do not forget that you can buy ready-made-up tape slings and thereby avoid using the tape knot.

BOWLINE WITH DOUBLE STOPPER

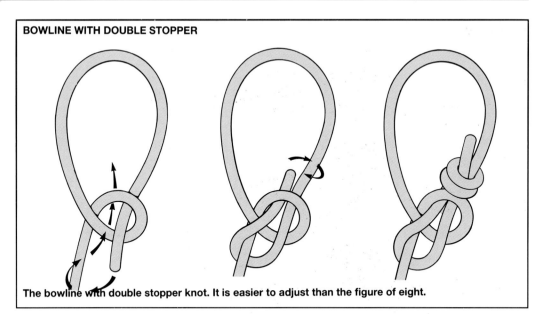

The bowline with double stopper knot. It is easier to adjust than the figure of eight.

PRUSIK KNOT

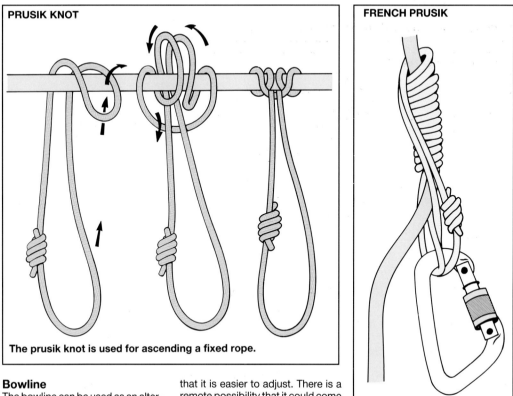

The prusik knot is used for ascending a fixed rope.

FRENCH PRUSIK

The French prusik can be released under load.

Bowline

The bowline can be used as an alternative to the figure eight for tying on to the end of the rope. Its main advantage over the figure eight is that it is easier to adjust. There is a remote possibility that it could come undone or work loose so always finish it off with a double stopper knot which should fit snugly up

THE USE OF BELAYS

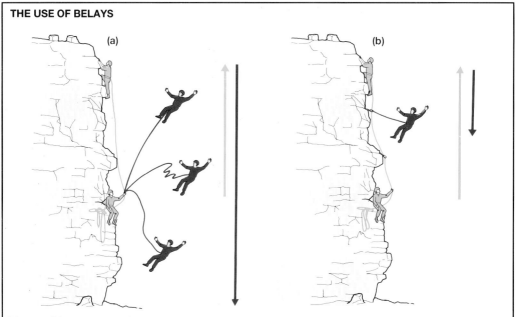

(a)

(b)

Diagram (a) shows the leader having run out 6 metres (20 feet) of rope but not having placed any running belays.

Diagram (b) shows the same situation but with a runner at 3 metres (10 feet). This reduces the length of fall

considerably. It is possible to achieve even lower fall factors on short falls with lots of rope paid out.

TAKING IN USING THE WAIST BELAY

This shows the sequence of taking in using the waist

belay. This is used when you have no belay plate. As with

the belay plate, never let go of the controlling rope.

against the bowline. It can be used for tying the rope directly around the waist if you find yourself without a harness.

Prusik knot

This knot is used for ascending a fixed rope (*see later* in this Chapter). Six millimetre (¼-inch) accessory

cord works most efficiently but, even so, it can still jam after being loaded. You must not subject it to a shock-loading or it will fail.

French prusik

Thisis a similar knot to the ordinary prusik but has the advantage that it can be released under load. This is

particularly useful when escaping from the system (*see* page 66). Soft 6-millimetre accessory cord works most efficiently.

FALL FACTOR

The **fall factor** is the term used to measure and describe the severity of a leader fall. It must be said from the outset that it is very much a theoretical measure, giving only a rough guide to the seriousness of a fall and the implications for the ropework system. It is a purely mathematical equation and does not take into consideration such things as the friction of the rope running through runners or over the rock. Neither does it take account of the shock-absorption properties of the climber's body. There are, however, some interesting facts that come out of the equation that have a bearing on the way in which runners are placed. The factor is arrived at by a simple equation.

$$\text{fall factor} = \frac{\text{total length of leader fall}}{\text{rope paid out by the second}}$$

Theoretically, the highest fall factor that the safety chain can cope with is 2. It is possible to achieve a figure higher than this but is beyond the scope of this book.

The illustration shows two separate leader falls. It is evident that a leader fall from only a few metres above the second can have serious repercussions and produce a high fall factor. It is, therefore, prudent to place running belays soon after leaving the stance. In a much longer fall, but one with more rope available to absorb the shock, there is considerably less strain on the system, although, of course, in a longer fall there is a much greater chance of hitting ledges and causing considerable damage to one's-self on the way down.

In *theory*, then, you would be well advised to place plenty of runners early on the pitch but to spread them out as you get further up the pitch. In practice, however, it is better to put plenty at the beginning and as many as you need or have left on your rack higher up.

EMERGENCY ROPE TECHNIQUES

Waist belay
Should the occasion arise where you find you have no belay plate or the facility to use an Italian hitch belay, you may need to safeguard

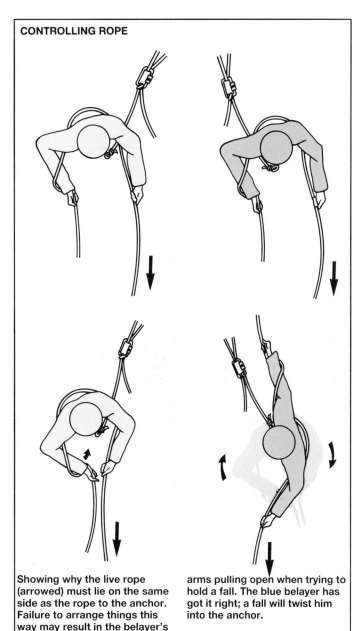

CONTROLLING ROPE

Showing why the live rope (arrowed) must lie on the same side as the rope to the anchor. Failure to arrange things this way may result in the belayer's arms pulling open when trying to hold a fall. The blue belayer has got it right; a fall will twist him into the anchor.

your partner's rope in another way. Until belay plates were developed all climbers used either a waist belay or, less commonly, a shoulder belay. Waist belays are far less efficient than belay plates and, in the wrong hands, lots of things

could go wrong. There are some important considerations: **1.** To have any hope of holding a severe fall, gloves must be worn. Long sleeves and padding around the back are also necessary. For instance, on a hot day where you are

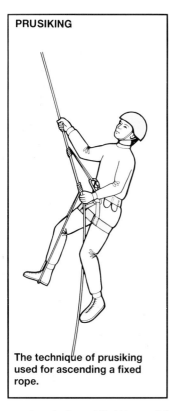

PRUSIKING

The technique of prusiking used for ascending a fixed rope.

wearing shorts and T-shirt, a waist belay is quite a risky technique to use.

2. When putting the rope around your waist, always loop it over your head.

3. Ensure that the live rope comes around on the same side as the rope to the anchor.

4. **Never** let go of the controlling or **dead** rope.

5. **Always** twist the 'dead' rope around the 'dead' arm – never around the 'live' arm.

There have been some terrible accidents caused by sloppy use of the waist belay – please take care to avoid such sloppiness.

PRUSIKING

This is the term used to describe the way in which to ascend a fixed rope using loops of cord, one for the foot and one to the sit-harness. There are many reasons why one might have to ascend a fixed rope. For example, it might be that you have

fallen off a traversing pitch and are suspended below an overhang where it is not possible to touch rock and regain the route by climbing the rock. You will obviously need to have practised the techniques before you get into that situation otherwise there is little hope of executing it successfully. Hanging a rope from a tree is an ideal way to gain practice and can even be good fun. You will need to experiment with the lengths of loop that you use but, as a rough guide, the sit-loop should be about 50 centimetres (20 inches) long and the foot one about 1.25 metres (4 feet). Remember, if they are too long, they can always be shortened but, if they are too short, you might not be able to lengthen them. The standard prusik knot is fine for prusiking but, on wet or muddy ropes, you may need to increase the holding power by putting in more turns. Note also that the French prusik could be used but be careful not to release it accidentally. The diagram shows a climber prusiking. Only one loop is moved at a time. The loop connected to the harness should always be above the foot loop for safety.

ESCAPING THE SYSTEM

This describes the way in which you can release yourself from the belay system and end of rope while ensuring the security of the climber you are responsible for. Take, for example, an emergency in which your partner has fallen and injured himself or herself, and you find it necessary for some reason to go down to your victim and render first aid or to go and get help while he or she stays in situ. Obviously, with a person's full weight hanging on the end of the rope it can be quite difficult to release from the belay plate and anchor system.

1. Tie off the belay plate to release both hands.

2. Put a French prussik on the load or live rope and clip it in back to your anchor point. If you cannot reach your anchors, you may have to put a second prusik on the ropes that tie you in to the anchor.

3. Release the belay plate and lower, slowly, the climber's weight

on to the French prusik.

4. Remove the climbing rope from the plate and immediately tie it with a figure eight knot back to a secure place on the anchor system.

5. You are now free to untie from the rope and do whatever may be necessary. If you have any doubts about whether the anchors are strong enough, do not hesitate to back them up.

It is really beyond the scope of this book to go much further than this but, for those who are interested, there is some recommended reading in the Further Reading list.

FALLING AND FAILING

Failure on a climb is inevitable from time to time. It happens to the best of climbers so there is no need to worry too much about it. Reasons for failure are numerous but, more commonly, it happens because you are on something that is too difficult for you, or it begins to rain and further ascent is impossible because of wet, greasy rock.

If a climb is too difficult for you, there is a chance that you might fall off it. This need not be quite as dreadful as it sounds, particularly if you have a running belay close by. With a runner above your head or just level with your waist, a 'fall' will hardly be noticed by either you or your second. Many climbers at the top end of the scale will fall repeatedly on to runners while trying to work out something that is extremely technical. Obviously, this requires great confidence in the placement of running belays and in your second's ability to hold the rope. It also requires a certain attitude of mind and not inconsiderable nerve. This technique of sieging a climb is called 'yo-yoing' and is not really recommended for beginners!

RETREATING FROM A CLIMB

If faced with the prospect of retreat, consider first whether it is possible for you to climb back down the pitch removing runners as you descend. This is known as 'reversing the climb'. If, however, you find the thought repellant you will certainly

ESCAPING FROM THE SYSTEM

(a)

(b)

(c)

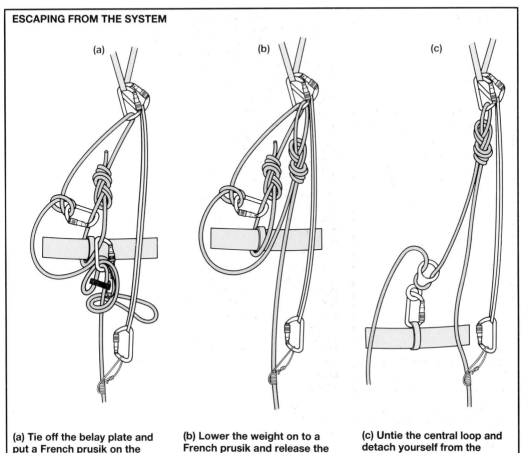

(a) Tie off the belay plate and put a French prusik on the live rope. Connect it back to the anchor.

(b) Lower the weight on to a French prusik and release the belay plate. Clip a figure eight into the anchor.

(c) Untie the central loop and detach yourself from the system. Prepare to descend on the spare rope.

have to lower down on the rope.

Suppose that you find yourself in-difficulty part way up a pitch and are contemplating retreat. The simple way is to leave your rope clipped through the highest runner (this should be level with or higher than your waist) and hang on the rope. You then allow your second to lower you back down to the stance using the top runner as the pulley point. As you descend, you must remember to remove the remaining running belays. On arrival at the stance, clip in to the belay anchor, untie from the end of the rope, and pull it through the runner. Unfortunately, this run-ner and its karabiner are now lost and, unless you go back to retrieve it at the earliest opportunity, you will

find that someone else will have gleefully added it to his or her rack!

It is very important to remember that, when lowering off in this man-ner, the rope should be clipped through the runner via a karabiner. **Never** lower off with the rope run-ning through a nylon sling because it will melt through the sling com-pletely and will almost certainly cause your death.

The above can only be done if you are less than half a rope's length from the stance. Should you find yourself higher up the pitch than that, you will either have to climb back down to a point where a lower is possible or, if you are using double rope technique, abseil off. This requires great care. To abseil,

you will have to untie from both ends of rope, thread them through the runner that you will use as the abseil anchor, and then knot them to-gether with a double fisherman's knot. Remember that, before you untie from the rope ends, you must clip yourself into something to safe-guard against a fall. Above all else, you must work quite carefully and methodically.

Once you are back on the stance, both you and your partner will have to retreat from the cliff. This may be a rather daunting prospect if you are three or four pitches up the climb, so again, exercise great caution and careful thought. Inevitably you will lose equipment but this is a small price to pay for a life.

CHAPTER 5

DESCENDING

Climbing down is never as easy as going up, but it is something that every climber must do. Many climbs finish at the top of cliffs that have very straightforward walking descents – little more than a care-free gambol back to the bottom and another climb. Occasionally, the descent requires a more careful approach than the climb itself: route finding may be difficult and there may even be graded rock climbing to descend.

If at all possible, you should try to face out from the rock because this will give you a much clearer picture of the problems that lie ahead. While, at times, this may seem insecure it is much speedier. If you come to a difficult section or feel particularly apprehensive you must then, obviously, turn around and face inwards but try to avoid becoming too stretched out because this inhibits movement and your view of handholds and footholds below. The same principles of balance and technique apply going down as going up. There will be occasions where the rope may be required for safety and protection. This can be used in a similar way to the way it was used during the climb, and each section of the descent can be treated as a pitch with the leader placing runners and arranging stances as necessary.

A speedier way of descending awkward or difficult terrain is by **abseil**, or **rappel**, as it is called in some countries. To descend by abseil, it is necessary to double the rope around an anchor point and go down on the doubled rope to a safe place. Once all the members of the party have got down, the rope can then be retrieved by pulling one end down and around the anchor point. In practice, this is not so easy as it sounds. There are many things that can go wrong with abseiling, and it is a sobering point to remember that

Abseiling off the Old Man of Hoy, Orkney Islands, Scotland. This is a speedy means of descent but must be carried out with care.

Left: Out to lunch! Practising abseiling techniques in a controlled situation is important. As in the case of the waist belay, sloppy abseiling technique can lead to serious injury or even death so make sure you know what you are doing.

Above: Abseiling without a safety rope but with a partner holding the bottom of the rope.

many well-known climbers have been killed in abseiling accidents – do not be one of them!.

Firstly, you should ensure that the anchor you choose is solid enough to take the full weight of the climber. This means that flakes or blocks of rock should be firmly attached to the face and should have no sharp edges. Any 'in-situ' slings or anchors should be in good condition and not cut or damaged in any way. If trees are available, they offer the best form of abseil anchor because they are often well rooted and make retrieving the rope a relatively easy task. It is very frustrating to drape the rope around a flake or block, make the descent, and then discover that the rope can not be retrieved because it is jammed at the anchor point. It is a good idea for the first person down to check that the rope will pull around the anchor. If it does not, then the person at the top of the abseil can make the necessary adjustments. Should you find yourself in this situation where the rope has jammed, do not climb back up the rope to free it unless you can use both ropes. Despite the cost of lost equipment, it may be necessary to sacrifice a sling or other item of gear to be absolutely certain that the rope can be retrieved.

ABSEILING TECHNIQUES

As with all climbing techniques, abseiling should be practised in a controlled situation before putting them to the test on a crag. There are many different abseiling devices available, all of which perform admirably, but may be extraneous and cumbersome items of equipment to carry. The simplest and most effective device is the figure-eight descendeur. This device generates a good deal of friction. Indeed, at the top of a long abseil, the weight of the rope hanging below will make it very difficult even to move. In the photograph we see the climber about to go over the edge. The rope that goes down the cliff, held in the right hand, is called the **controlling rope.** The speed of descent is regulated by the climber allowing the rope to slide through the controlling hand at a rate that feels most comfortable. Be careful if you go fast, because it is quite possible to burn your hand severely, even to the point of not being able to grip the rope. The left hand is not required for controlling speed. It is, however, useful to hold the ropes above the device for stability. Many people grip much too tightly with this hand. There is no need.

The most difficult part of any abseil is getting over the edge. Once you are on your way, the rest is normally very straightforward, provided you do not have to go over any obstacles en route. Keep the feet apart and the legs straight. Do not let the feet drop too far below your bottom as they will most likely slip and you will fall on your face. Whatever happens, it is vital that you do not let go of the controlling rope. When practising for the first time, it may be prudent to have someone operating a safety line. Usually you abseil in the line that the rope hangs in but, if you need to move diagonally at any time, do so with caution because, if you slip, there will be a long pendulum and this could lead

A long, free abseil into Parliament House Cave at Gogarth, North Wales. A retreat may involve a long prusik back.

ABSEIL DEVICE

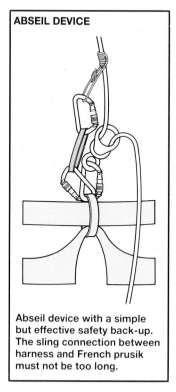

Abseil device with a simple but effective safety back-up. The sling connection between harness and French prusik must not be too long.

to all sorts of problems, not least injury.

Overhangs can be awkward to negotiate. If the anchor is a good one and your nerves are sound, stand on the lip and jump out. As you do so, allow the rope to slide reasonably fast and, by the time you swing back in, you should be well past the lip. Be careful not to trap fingers or clothing between rock and rope. If you are uncertain about that technique, abseil down to the lip and lie sideways against the rock with the controlling hand outermost. Lower yourself gradually over the edge, taking care not to trap the fingers of your balance hand as you go over.

Before beginning the descent, it is important to make sure that the rope hangs all the way to the ground or to a suitable ledge. When throwing the rope down the cliff, make sure that you coil it into neat coils in the hand so that it unravels itself without tangling. Unfortunately, snags and tangles often occur and it may be necessary to sort them out as you

go down. You must never abseil below a tangle or snag in the hope that you can pull the rope free from below. If you are unable to free it, you will have to climb back up and this will cause all sorts of problems. Stop well above the offending obstacle and lock off the device allowing you to use both hands to manipulate the rope.

Locking off can be effected in a variety of ways. The system described below can be used to lock off any device used, and so it is the only method that need be in your repertoire. Wrap the controlling rope around the thigh about three or four times, making sure that you do not let go of the rope as you are doing it and also that the turns are high up the leg. It should now be possible to let go without descending any further. Any problems with snags or tangles can now be dealt with using both hands.

Abseil safety

When you are practising the techniques, it would be wise to use a safety line on the first few descents. This can be done by a partner using a belay plate. Make sure that he or she is well anchored so that, if necessary, he/she can hold all of your body weight. Once you get out on to the crag, however, a safety line will be out of the question. It is possible to go down with a safety back-up on the rope. The illustration shows the French prusik being used for this task. The French prusik is tied around both ropes, and the ends are clipped to a screwgate karabiner which, in turn, is clipped via a short sling to the harness. As the abseiler descends, the prusik is dragged down by the balance hand. If for some unavoidable reason, you let go of the ropes completely, the French prusik will jam, thereby halting further descent. It is vitally important that two factors are observed.
1. When hanging from the safety sling, the knot must remain within arm's reach.
2. There must be enough turns in the French prusik to hold the weight.

The French prusik is by far the most efficient knot to use for this purpose because it can be released

easily while the load is on it. This safety system is ideal for the person who descends first, particularly in situations where problems may arise because what is below is not known.

For any other people descending, it is enough to hold the bottom of the abseil rope and, if you see that the person is having some difficulty or has lost control of the rope, you can simply pull hard on the rope and any further descent will be halted. Regardless of how experienced you might become, you would always be wise to remember this aspect of abseil safety.

Other methods of abseiling

The figure-of-eight descendeur is probably the most commonly used device but it does have one major drawback. It can only be used for abseiling. If weight is not a problem and the descent requires many abseils, by all means consider carrying a figure of eight, but you will have to put up with it dangling around uselessly while you are doing things other than abseiling. The belay plate can be used as an abseiling device. It does, however, tend to be quite 'jerky' in the control of the descent but, nonetheless, it is very effective. An extra karabiner can be inserted alongside the main karabiner. This reduces the tendency of the plate to grab and therefore leads to a smoother descent. A word of warning here, though. If you are abseiling on two ropes, of unequal thickness or different textures, joined together there is a tendency for one to slide through the plate more quickly than the other. This causes the rope to creep around the anchor, and the ends may then be of unequal length and one rope reaches safety but the other does not. In this situation, continuing to abseil past the end of one rope will have fatal consequences because your weight comes on to a single rope and it pulls around the anchor. You should make every attempt to prevent this situation from happening and, by tying the loose ends together in a firm knot, the chances of sliding off the end of one or even both ropes are greatly minimized.

KARABINER BRAKES

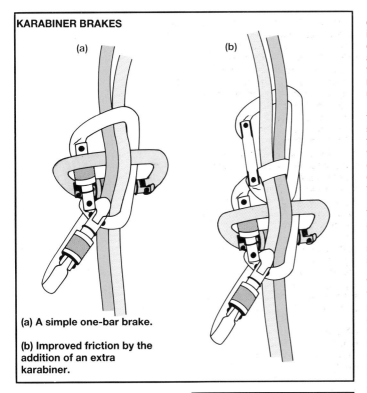

(a)

(b)

(a) A simple one-bar brake.

(b) Improved friction by the addition of an extra karabiner.

Karabiner brakes

A karabiner brake is very useful for abseiling because it makes use of equipment which is normally carried by the rock climber. However it can be set up incorrectly.

The illustrations show a simple brake using one karabiner as a brake bar, and a simple method for increasing the friction of the device. Be sure to use screwgate karabiners wherever possible, or double up on snaplinks so that the gates open in opposite directions.

The availability of screwgate karabiners may be limited, in which case, two will suffice. Use one to extend the brake away from the harness so as to avoid the situation where the rope can rub on the harness and the other to set up the brake-bar support krab. The brake bar itself can be of double snaplinks.

Italian hitch

The Italian hitch, the sliding friction knot mentioned in Chapter 4, can be used as an abseil device. Unfortunately, it does tend to twist ropes very badly, often resulting in a

change in the handling characteristics of the rope. It twists the inner core of the rope within the sheath, and it becomes twisted in a different way to that of manufacture. The rope may then become totally unmanageable for the rest of its use.

If you are abseiling on a single fixed rope using the hitch, make sure that all the twists can fall out of the end of the rope by stretching the whole rope out below you. On double ropes, treat the two ropes as one and put on a single hitch using the two ropes. If you were to use an Italian hitch on both ropes, they tend to twist around each other below and become badly tangled. Remember that a large pear-shaped karabiner is by far the most suitable for use with Italian hitches.

The classic abseil

The classic abseil is included only as an emergency option should you ever find yourself in a situation where no equipment is available. It is certainly not a very satisfactory method of abseiling because it is uncomfortable for long distances. Padding or strong clothing should be worn with particular regard to protecting the shoulder and inside the leg. On 'free' abseils, where it is not possible to touch rock, it is particularly uncomfortable. It is also very easy to set it up incorrectly with disastrous consequences. You should also be well recommended only to consider using it on double ropes.

To set up the classic abseil, stand astride the rope and reach down behind you with your right hand. Pull the rope up and across your chest, over the head and left shoulder, and down your back into the right hand (for left-handed people, simply work the opposite way). The friction generated is enough to allow you to control the rope and speed of descent easily. For more comfort during use, twist yourself slightly rightwards (left for left handers) and lead with the right foot. If, at any time, it is necessary to step over an overlap or overhang or any obstacle, lead with the right foot (left for left-handers), otherwise the rope around the inside of the leg may ride up around the knee causing you to flip upside down.

CLASSIC ABSEIL

The classic abseil. Make sure your wear plenty of padding.

CHAPTER 6

CLIMBING BETTER

To improve your climbing, there is no substitute for actual climbing experience and a desire to ascend harder and more taxing climbs. Rock climbing is not just a physical sport, and often, a delicate and precise approach to the climb will succeed where muscle and brute strength would fail. There is an element of science about runner placements and rope management, and then, of course, there is the psychological aspect: the fear, the worry,

the tension, failure, and success. These are all essential elements that go into making the sport so addictive. There are few training regimes that can cover all these aspects, but climbing itself provides them all.

Often, climbers will not do very much during the cold, wet winter months and so, when the first days of spring arrive and fingers yearn for the feel of warm sun-kissed rock, climbers are mentally and physically unprepared for the coming season.

Below left: Feats of strength are performed in the most bizarre situations. Here the penalty for failure is a good ducking.

Below: Bouldering quite close to the ground is one of the most pleasant ways to train for climbing. Problems that may be too hard 30 metres (100 feet) up can be attempted without having to worry about ropes and other equipment.

To begin with, then, it may be better to assure yourself of a few successes and not expect to take up where you left off last season. There is nothing more depressing than going out on to the first climb of the year and failing miserably on a route for which you are not prepared. It is more important initially to establish your feelings about rock climbing, to rediscover the pleasure it gives. With that comes the desire to climb more and, ultimately, the physical fitness to climb better. Not everyone is a natural climber, but with proper preparation, thousands of people can be good climbers.

The concept of specific training for climbing is relatively new – ten years old – although it would be foolish to say that climbers have only recently started to train for climbing. What have changed are the attitudes to training. These changes took place in the mid-1970s. Prior to that, time-train-ing took place on boulders, bridges, buildings, and by performing great feats of strength or agility to prove prowess. All of these still exist today and are as much a part of rock climbing as the rock climbs themselves but, additionally, there is a kind of clinical approach adopted by the established elite and by the up-and-coming young climbers of the day. Spurred on by media exposure, glossy climbing magazines, and the opportunity to be sponsored by

manufacturers, there is a race to be 'the best'. Ten years ago, the hardest climbs may not have been repeated for years; nowadays, climbs are lucky if they last a day before they are overcome again.

CLIMBING WALLS

The 'orange-juice-only-and-climbing-walls-four-nights-a-week' regime of the mid-1970s still exists today, although it is refreshing to see beer in place of orange juice occasionally, but only if a fifth or sixth night is spent on the wall or in the multigym. The potential of training for climbing is epitomized by one significant episode in British climbing history. In the mid-1970s, a climbing wall was opened in Leeds University. It was not an elaborate one by modern standards, but adequate. The achievements of one person on this wall astounded protagonists of the sport and, after a winter of climbing on the wall, he transferred his talents to rock, repeating many of the hardest climbs of the day and adding harder ones of his own. What is more remarkable is that until he climbed on the wall he had never climbed before. Today there are some 250 climbing walls throughout the United Kingdom, and thousands more around the world. They vary considerably in style and suitability. Some are designed by experts;

Above: Climbing walls are the ideal way to train during long, cold, and wet winter months.

Right: Bouldering. Make sure that you take a partner along to spot you in case you fall.

others by enthusiastic climbers. Unfortunately, what is a good wall for beginners is not necessarily a good wall for training the best.

Some climbing walls offer the facility for roped climbing, but most climbers who visit walls opt to discard ropes and climb only with rock shoes and chalk bag. A newcomer to rock climbing might find it an odd experience to walk in on a group of climbers practising on a wall. Often, they will spend an entire session trying to work out one problem which may only involve three or four moves up the wall and then, once it is solved, they might try and eliminate a hold to make it even more difficult. On paper, it sounds bizarre, but problems such as these are undertaken with great enthusiasm. Problem solving is an enjoyable way to train on walls and, for most climbers, it is the only way to make it tolerable. A more clinical approach is adopted by some and may involve a planned circuit or traverse of the wall without touching the ground. This circuit should include a great variety of moves, handholds, footholds, and resting positions; it is probably a more effective way of training because strength, stamina, and muscle endurance are increased. Traverses are sometimes only a few centimetres off the ground, and some such moves may be impossible for tall people, particularly if the only handholds you are allowed to use are low down, too.

BOULDERING

Bouldering is a much more satisfying way to train for climbing and, for some, it is an end in itself. Nothing gives greater pleasure or satisfaction than to visit some boulders in a grassy meadow and attempt problems that may be just beyond your capabilities knowing that the chances of being injured are very slim. Success can have far-reaching consequences to your attitude to climbing. For example, some years ago, a boulder problem was discovered which, by the nature of the rock, had obviously never been climbed. The gauntlet had been thrown down. The problem involved moving from a precarious balance position,where one finger in a side pull was all that would hold the climber, across a slightly overhanging wall to a good

side hold out of sight on the other side. Unfortunately, the only grip between was a tiny finger hold at full stretch. After an hour, we were no further advanced on solving the problem than we were when we started. We were irritated that we had not been able to solve such an apparently trivial problem, not much more than a metre off the ground. After dinner, some talking, some thinking, and two muscle-aching, finger-ripping hours later, our determination had brought us success. Now, with the sequence of moves firmly implanted in mind and body, it has become a pièce de résistance, the ideal way to test the unwary visitor.

Bouldering with a group of friends is the most rewarding way to go, especially if everyone is compatible in terms of ability. It becomes quite competitive, in a friendly way of course, and the banter is good. It is interesting how unwritten rules emerge. For instance, once you have had a try and fallen off, it is off to the back of the queue to await your turn. Someone will get a little further than the others and this spurs people to try harder, and eventually the problems are solved. Then, of course, it is not always the case that there is only one way to tackle a problem. Climbers will climb a section of rock in different ways depending on strength, technique, agility, and even height. There are some problems that are impossible for short people because they literally cannot reach the holds. If that is the case, admit defeat and walk away or perfect the 'dyno' technique.

BUILDINGS AND OTHER STRUCTURES

The inventiveness of climbers to create problems out of the most bizarre situations is astounding:

A very hard climb will require much strength, stamina, and technique. The ability and nerve to make continuous moves up steep or overhanging rock hanging on by finger tips can only be gained through practice.

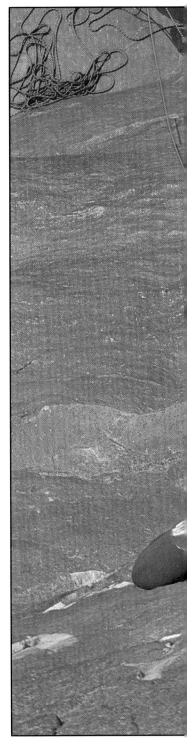

pull-ups on door lintels, traverses across brick edges; mantleshelves on window ledges. Castles, railway bridges, houses have all given climbers good sport over the years and will most certainly continue to do so in the future. But always make sure you have the owner's permission to climb.

SPECIFICS ABOUT TRAINING

Unless you aspire to achieve great things in the climbing world and become one of the top performers, it is probably not worth becoming too intense about training. There is no doubt, however, that training in any form is bound to be beneficial to overall performance. Because climbing is such a good form of training for climbing, any other training schedule needs to incorporate all the different elements. Broadly speaking they can be categorized as follows:
1. Overall fitness and stamina.
2. Strength and mobility.
3. Skill and attitude.

Overall fitness and stamina
To sustain long periods of exertion, overall cardio-vascular fitness is of paramount importance. Activities, such as running or cycling, are ideal. For the more clinically minded, try easy, repetitive weights circuits at a fairly brisk rate and/or easy traverses on a wall returning to the ground periodically to recover. Basically, anything that makes you out of breath and work hard will do.

Strength and mobility
Strength increases your confidence in your ability. Upper body strength should be developed fairly scientifically to avoid tendon and muscle injury. You should be particularly careful when building up finger strength because the joints and tendons are very prone to long-term damage. Warming up properly is the key to success. You will rarely need to use enormous amounts of strength in climbing, so build up muscle endurance by 'progressive-overload' training (gradually increasing the amount of work done). Mobility or suppleness can play an important role in climbing;

although the very best performers have a certain level of natural mobility, this can be improved further by stretching exercises. Again, warming up is particularly important in stretching, and at least a twenty-minute warm-up is necessary before proper stretching can begin. Yoga is used by some people to enhance flexibility.

and actually getting into that position could require careful planning of the sequence to be used. Some people have a natural ability to do this but, for many, experience and training are the only ways to achieve success.

Above all, attitude is important. The desire to achieve and motivation for climbing in the first place are paramount. Having established that you want to climb, the next problem is to prepare yourself mentally for the undertaking, Read about the climbs, talk to people, look at the route. Try to imagine yourself on the rockface, and approach the climb confident that at least you are going to give it your very best effort. Once you are on the climb, you will certainly experience much emotion, apprehension, elation, fear, moments of tranquillity, anger, frustration, and hopefully a sense of accomplishment. Controlling all of these takes a lot of effort. If you allow some of the emotion to run amok, it has a cataclysmic effect on the rest of your performance. Strength and skill wane rapidly in the face of uncontrolled fear, leading ultimately to certain failure on the climb.

OBSERVE, IMAGINE EMULATE

Today there are many thousands of 'good' climbers around. They are people who are prepared to put in some effort to achieve. There are also, as in other sports, some exceptional performers. These are people who are a joy to behold as they effortlessly ascend a piece of rock that had previously reduced you to a nervous wreck. Each climber has a distinctive style, be it the way he/she climbs or the mental approach. Watch these people; try to imagine how it feels to do those moves, and then try yourself. Perhaps one day you too will become the world's finest climber.

Skill and attitude

Skill only comes with practice, so the obvious form of training is climbing itself, on walls, boulders, or anything that gives similar movements.

Working out moves or problems can become something of a science. For example, to complete a particular problem may necessitate a certain hold to be used in a specific way,

CHAPTER 7

ROCK FOR CLIMBING

Fortunately for rock climbers, the world is not short of rock for climbing: limestone gorges; great granite cliffs; gritstone edges; bastions of basalt; bluffs of rough, red sandstone; low round boulders at Fontainebleau in France; towering jagged heights of the Italian Dolomites, soaring walls of Yosemite, of Romsdal, and, mightiest perhaps of all, of the Baltoro Cathedrals in the Himalayas. And, whenever there is rock, there is climbing. It would be impossible to conduct a detailed world tour within this book but, to whet the appetite, here is a brief country-by-country survey of some of the best climbing in the world.

BRITISH ISLES

Britain has been blessed with a complex geology that has furnished its small area with a great variety of climbing rock.

Devon has sea cliffs on north and south coasts; Baggy Point in the north and Berry Head in the south

are, perhaps, the most spectacular. The county also has great inland climbs, on volcanic rock at Dewerstone and the Dartmoor tors, and on white limestone at Chudleigh near Exeter.

Moving further north into Derbyshire, Lancashire, and Yorkshire – some might say into the heart of British climbing – there are important limestone and gritstone cliffs. Sometimes, little more than outcrops, for many they are the only crags in the world. Certainly, in world terms some very important and spectacular developments have taken place on crags such as High Tor, Millstone, and Stanage.

Below: 'Great Western', an HVS climb at Chudleigh Rocks, Devon.

Overleaf left: 'A Dream of White Horses', a seacliff climb on Gogarth, North Wales.

Overleaf right: 'Debauchery' on High Tor, Matlock, Derbyshire.

West of the Peak District, as it is called, are the more traditional, though equally important, cliffs of Wales. In the south, there are the seacliffs of the Pembrokeshire coastline and, in the north, mountain crags, roadside crags, and the world-famous seacliffs of Gogarth. Clogwyn du'r Arddu is one of the mountain crags steeped in history and anecdote; the cliffs of the Llanberis Pass and the classic climbs of the Ogwen Valley are other places where many famous names have carved their reputations and left their indelible marks.

In the north-west, there is the Lake District, land of Wordsworth and stomping ground of early pioneers such as O G Jones and the Abraham brothers. Mighty, remote mountain crags on Scafell and Gable, are the domain of ravens and hardened mountaineers while, in the more accessible valleys of Borrowdale and Langdale, rock climbers can practise their craft in close proximity to roads or easy-access footpaths.

Scotland's cliffs are among the most impressive in Britain. An infinite variety of crags, from sea stacks and seacliffs to 300-metre-plus (1000-foot) routes on Ben Nevis, the highest summit in the United Kingdom. For the roadside 'crag rat', there is little to satiate the appetite but, for those with a sense of adventure and some mountaineering knowledge, there is more than a lifetime's-worth of climbing to be had.

The most significant cliffs in Scotland are Carn Dearg on Ben Nevis and Carnmore, beyond Loch Maree in the wild and remote north-west of the country, which is approached by either a walk or, for the amphibious, a short canoe trip and a slightly lesser walk. But, by whichever approach, the reward for the effort is magnificent climbing on a spectacular crag in the most wonderful surroundings that you are

Far left: The Napes Needle. This is where it all began in 1886.

Left: 'Valkyrie' a classic HVS climb on Gritstone, Froggat Edge, Derbyshire.

ever likely to behold – a five-star expedition.

In the bleak Cairngorm massif, the Shelterstone Crag rises high and mighty for some 275 metres (900 feet) above lonely Loch Avon. Other great Highland venues are Glencoe on the west coast, where such bastions as the Rannoch Wall on Buchaille Etive Mor, and the West Face of Aonach Dubh arrest the gaze. Not too far away, by Fort William, the Poldubh crags are, fast gaining as a cragrats' playground.

The biggest mountain crags of all in Scotland, however, are to be found at Craig an Dubh Loch, where routes in excess of 300 metres (1000 feet) are not uncommon. A bigger cliff, still, rises sheer from the sea for well over 350 metres (1200 feet) at St Johns Head in the Orkneys, far to the north. Unfortunately, its majesty is rather flawed by crumbling rock.

Much better climbing is to be found on the adjacent sea stack of the Old Man of Hoy, which is the most impressive of all of the Scottish sea stacks – another worthwhile expedition. The Old Man of Hoy exemplifies the special problems of climbing on sea cliffs, which are those of access, tides, retreat, and predatory seabirds – the odiferous Fulmar is just about the last thing a climber would want to meet.

When visiting a sea cliff, you would be well advised to take careful note of the times of the tides. High tides may mean that access to the start of the climb is difficult or even impossible and a retreat, once you have embarked on the climb, is equally so. Climbing at your limit, with the sea or the dark snatching at your heels, may be exciting, but it is not the best way to enjoy the ambience of coastal crags.

Salt air plays havoc with alloy-based equipment – karabiners, chocks, and the like – and these should be washed in fresh water after two or three visits. Should you or your equipment be unfortunate enough to suffer full immersion in the sea itself, then a thorough dousing in fresh water is advised.

'Ardverikie wall', a splendid climb in a lovely Scottish setting.

Left: An idyllic evening climb in Pembrokeshire, Wales. The climbers are on 'Richochet', a fine climb on St Govan's Head.

Below: The Gorges du Verdon, southern France. A climbers' paradise: long, hot days; fine, solid limestone and 300-metre (1000-foot) climbs.

EUROPE

Arguably, France has the best, certainly the best-known, climbing rock in Europe, from the superb limestone of the Vercors near Grenoble, and the Gorge du Verdon nearer the Mediterranean to the low, round boulders of Fontainebleau near Paris. Between are the Alps where

excellent rock climbing can be found, although other mountaineering skills may need to be employed to gain access to the climbs proper because there are glaciers and snow fields to cross. This is definitely not 'crag rat' country!

The Vercors and the Gorge du Verdon offer superb climbing on soaring, steep, limestone walls,

Left: Jon de Montjoye leading 'Sidermek', a 6c climb in the Frimes et Chatiments area.

Above: The 'Symphonie d'Autumn', a climb on compact limestone near Briançon, France.

Overleaf: Jon de Montjoye seconding the crux pitch of an 8a climb, 'La Crysalis'.

some of which are up to 500 metres (1650 feet) long. The climate in the Verdon is excellent for most of the year, but winters are cold and snowy and the height of summer can be unbearably hot with temperatures up to and occasionally exceeding 40°C! In those sorts of temperatures you either go for a swim or you sunbathe.

For the real rock 'guru', perhaps the best rock of all for climbing is at Boux which has sun, meadows, wine, and the roughest, firmest limestone imaginable – a climber's paradise. The rock of the alpine regions is generally granite, and around Chamonix, Mont Blanc, it is a particularly fine species. Coarse, rough, and of a splendid orange-yellow colour, it is a joy to climb on. Climbs, such as the South Face of

the Aiguille du Midi, have become justifiably popular with visitors from all over the world. Unfortunately, it is only a hop, skip, and a jump from the cable car and, even though crampons and ice axe are required to get to the start of the climb, one has to get up early to avoid the crowds.

Further north in France there is the once very popular limestone of Saussois. Of perhaps greater significance nowadays are the boulders of Fontainebleau. This is an area of forest near to Paris, and scattered around throughout the region are huge numbers of boulders varying in size but rarely more than 5 metres (15 feet) high. The importance of this bouldering area, one of the most prolific in the world, ranks high with Parisian climbers, and many fine and testing problems exist. There are coloured circuits marked out in parts of the forest, and it is a fit and able climber who can complete them on a first visit.

Spain is rapidly gaining popularity as a vast rock climber's playground, and one with plenty of rock yet to discover. It is said that once her treasures have been displayed fully, Spain will be the world's pre-eminent climbing-rock nation. Many of the important climbing areas are situated close to the Costa del Sol.

Crags, such as Montanejos and the Pénon d'Ifach near Calpe, offer quality climbing on excellent limestone. Not far from Pamplona, where the infamous stampede takes place, are the crags of Echauri. Further north, the Picos de Europa is the oldest and perhaps best-known climbing region.

In Norway, there are huge granite and grabbro walls and slabs everywhere – many of them unclimbed. The Troll Wall is perhaps the most famous, or infamous.

In Italy there are the limestone cliffs of the Dolomites, not all solid, but still offering a unique experience.

In Saxony, Czechoslovakia, and Yugoslavia there are sandstone crags and pinnacles.

Malcolm Campbell climbing on a recently developed wall below the Mirroir de Fou area. Route unknown; grade 6c.

NORTH AMERICA

As you would expect in so vast a continent, North America holds an outstanding array of climbing areas. Some of them are justly world famous and some, arguably, the world's best. Of these, Yosemite, in California, a great glacier-gouged valley with 1000-metre (3300-foot) granite walls, is probably the best known. There are, however, many other equally fine climbing areas: Joshua Tree; Boulder, Colorado; Red Rocks, Las Vegas; Squamish Chief in Vancouver; Shawangunks over on the east; Cathedral, White-horse, and Cannon in New Hampshire. In the deserts of Utah, there are huge sandstone climbs in gorges, on pinnacles, and on remote outcrops. Multiday routes, too, abound in the Black Canyon of the Gunnison, a place to rival the

biggest and best of anywhere in the world.

Multi-day routes, too, abound in the Black Canyon of the Gunnison, a place to rival the biggest and best of anywhere in the world.

'Big wall' climbing poses many problems for the uninitiated and the

Below: The grandeur of Yosemite Valley. The mighty prow on the left is that of El Capitan, home of some of the world's finest and hardest rock climbs. The climbs stretch for kilometres with firm granite classics on every crag.

Overleaf right: Middle Cathedral, a majestic 2000 foot bastion in Yosemite Valley California.

Overleaft left: A Tyrolean traverse fromthe top of the Lost Arrow Spire in Yosemite, California, United States.

experienced alike. A climb, such as the Nose of El Capitan in Yosemite Valley, California, can be climbed by a strong team of two climbers moving lightweight in two days. At the other end of the spectrum, some teams, even given perfect weather conditions, can take up to four or five days. it is not enough on such climbs to be a good climber. Skilful rope handling, problem-free route-finding, and a calm and controlled mental approach, are all attributes necessary for a successful climb.

The decision about whether or not to go for a fast, lightweight ascent of a big wall can be a particularly difficult one to make. You may decide to commit yourself totally to the climb and take nothing more than is required – climbing gear and some food and water. Moving in such a lightweight manner gives you every chance of moving quickly but, if you get caught out by the weather, or lose the route, or have any kind of 'epic', you may spend a very uncomfortable night out. On the other hand, taking too much equipment, food and water, clothing, and sleeping gear may mean that you spend an unjustifiable length of time on the route, most of which will be spent hauling an enormous sack full of gear up the rock face – a most unpleasant climbing experience!

It is really beyond the scope of this basic manual to discuss 'big wall' techniques in any great detail, but there are some appropriate recommendations under 'Further Reading'.

AUSTRALIA AND NEW ZEALAND

There are those, and they are not all Australians, who may claim that the world's best rock-climbing playground is Arapiles, with its perfect rock and permanent sun. Truth to tell it probably is, but it is certainly

Far left: Bill Wayman climbing on 'Triples', Seneca Rocks, in the United States.

Left: Bill Wayman climbing on Colorado Rock in the USA.

not the only place to go climbing in Australia. Not far away from Arapiles is the Grampian range of mountains, an area that boasts an infinite number of classic climbs. The rough and intimidating granite of Mount Buffalo offers a respite from the searing heat of Arapiles in the summer, and elsewhere in the country there is climbing just outside Canberra at Booroomba rocks and further north on the seacliffs near Sydney, and again not far away the Blue Mountains. In the Flinders Range, just north of Adelaide in South Australia, is Moonarie, reputed to come a close second to Arapiles for the title 'Best Crag in the World'.

New Zealand is more a land of mountaineers than rock climbers, but that is not to say that the country is without some fine climbing. In the deep south of the South Island are the perfect granite cliffs of the Darran Mountains. In the Mount Cook region, there are some good, though somewhat loose rock climbs

on peaks, such as Malte Brun and Mount Walter. For the 'crag rat', there are the bluffs near the airport or, a few hours' drive away near Christchurch, there is Castle Rock.

In the North Island, by far the most important climbing area is that of Whanganui Bay on the shores of the magnificent and scenic Lake Taupo. Though short, the climbs here possess allure and good quality, and lots of sunshine all the year round.

Right: 'Birdman', a grade 23 climb at Arapiles in Australia. This cliff is one of the most important crags in the world, and one on which climbing standards are being stretched. Below: A broad grin says it all! This is Whanganui Bay on North Island, New Zealand. The climb is 'Sayonara', described in the guide as a 'splendid handcrack', and one of dozens of superb routes in the delightful rock climbing playground.

OTHER WORLD AREAS

As we have said, there is rock for climbing the world over, and the list given here is significant only for those areas we have, perforce, omitted; South Africa's Table Mountain; Mount Kenya's beautiful mountain rock climbs; the sandstone jewels of Jordan's Wadi Tame; the many crags of Japan; the few of Hong Kong; the hundreds of metres of black granite rearing from the jungle to the summit of Kinabalu in Borneo; Grecian rock; Maltese rock; Baffin Island and Baltoro rock; rock and more rock: all for climbing.

There is no 'best rock' for climbing although, of the sedimentary rocks, limestone habitually offers fine routes, and lovers of limestone will tell you it is the best rock for climbing. But then lovers of Derbyshire's Peak District gritstone will make the same claim for their rock, and certainly gritstone makes for grand climbs. Other igneous rock is good, too: granite and gabbro are especially given to great routes. All of the skills described in this book work on all kinds of rock, although climbing styles may need to be modified slightly from one rock type to another. For example, gritstone favours masters of the jam; on limestone, strong fingers are useful; while, on the granite slabs of Yosemite's Glacier Apron, a long neck goes a long way. These varieties of texture and size and surface and shape, and the way in which climbing techniques have to be adapted or modified are all part of the great richness that makes rock climbing such a consumingly absorbing sport. For many climbers, it is enough to spend their lives climbing in their own country, and many countries have more than a lifetime's climbing in them but, for those with greater aspirations there are rich experiences to be gained the world over.

Right: A climb at Moonarie, South Australia.

Far right: 'Hangman', a grade 19 climb on Castle Rock near Christchurch, New Zealand.

CHAPTER 8

GUIDEBOOKS AND GRADING SYSTEMS

One of the problems confronting a beginner is where to find the nearest rock and, once it has been found, discovering where exactly the routes go. The best way to find where the rock is is to ask at your local outdoor retailer, or in Britain, to write to the British Mountaineering Council who, among other things, will also be able to give you details of your nearest climbing club should you wish to join one. Clubs are good places to meet climbing partners, as well as sources of general information and social forums, too. Browsing through the monthly climbing publications, such as *Climber* or *High*, will add greatly to your general climbing knowledge, furnish yet more information and, with luck, prove to be a source of light entertainment or even amusement. *See also* 'Further Reading'.

Finding a route on a crag is easy – at least, in theory. Most crags of any significance, in most climbing nations, are described in some guidebook. Some crags are subjects for whole guidebooks, while other guidebooks embrace a group of crags in an area; and then there are guidebooks which give details of every single known route within its scope while others offer a selection of routes that are generally considered to appeal, from a wider area.

Britain probably has the most

Right: Filming taking place on a Welsh classic, 'Mojo' (E1 5b) at Craig y Forwyn. This is a steep limestone crag.

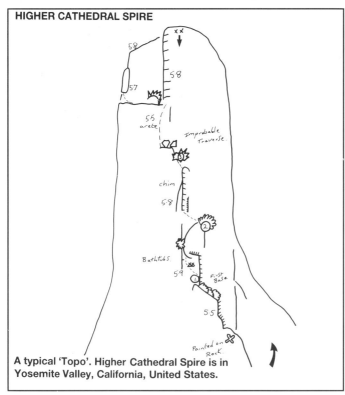

HIGHER CATHEDRAL SPIRE

A typical 'Topo'. Higher Cathedral Spire is in Yosemite Valley, California, United States.

comprehensive range of guide-books of all the climbing countries, although France and the United States cannot be far behind. A typical guidebook might encompass the following information: some historical notes; first-aid and accident procedure; details of the whereabouts of campsites; access roads, huts, paths; and, of course, the crags themselves. Some guidebooks contain additional information on flora, fauna, and geology.

A guidebook is very much what the author makes it, and there are good and bad. Most will carry an explanation of that area's or that country's grading system, and some will also use a star reference, from one to three, to indicate routes of special quality. Routes themselves may be accorded a written description, or simply shown by topographical drawings ('topos') or by lines drawn on photographs of the crag, or by a combination of two or all of these things.

Written descriptions vary, according to the author's taste, from spare, prosaic notes to eloquent tracts of near-poetical fancy; some are clinical, others joyful; some are serious, others humorous; some give a hold-by-hold description of every move, '. . . using a good right handjam and a small foothold out to the left, make a long reach to a . . .'; others only the most general of indications, '. . . continue generally upwards for another 300 metres . . .'. In the end, however, they all do much the same job – getting you to the bottom of the route of your choice. Nearly all guidebooks will tell you how hard and how long a route is, and many will do the same for each of that route's constituent pitches.

The tradition is that a route is named by whoever climbed it first, and it is likely to have been graded by that person, too, although the grade may be subject to later revision when more people climbed it. The name usually sticks. Like guidebooks, tastes in route names vary, from the mundane to the exotic, for example: Right Eliminate, Ordinary Route, the Naked Edge, Ride the Wild Surf, Cockblock, Comes the Dervish, Raped by Affection, Hitler's Buttock, Cardiac Arête, Pilier de l'Arab Demante. The list and scope are endless.

There is, of course, nothing to stop you turning up at a crag and,

Rock Climbing Grades

UK	UIAA*	EAST GERMANY	CZECHO-SLOVAKIA	FRANCE	USA	AUSTRALIA
MODERATE	III				5.0	4
DIFFICULT	III+				5.1	5
HARD DIFFICULT	IV–				5.2	6
VERY DIFFICULT	IV				5.3	7
HARD VERY DIFFICULT	IV+				5.4	8, 9
MILD SEVERE	–V–				5.5	10, 11
V			4c	5.6	12, 13
V+	VIIa	VI	5a	5.7	14
VI–	VIIb	VII	5b	5.8	15
VI	VIIc	VIIa	5c	5.9	16 / 17
VI+					
VII–	VIIIa	VIIb	6a	5.10 a b c d	18 / 19 / 20 / 21
VII	VIIIb	VIIc			
	VIIIc		6b		
VII+					
VIII–	IXa		6c	5.11 a b c	22 / 23 / 24
VIII	IXb				
VIII+	IXc		7a		25
IX–	Xa		7b	5.12	26 / 27
IX					28 / 29
IX+			7c		30
X–					
X			8a	5.13	

*Union Internationale des Associations Alpines

ignoring all that the guidebook counsels, climb anywhere and everywhere you can, or choose. There are those, though they are few, who, scorning all convention, do just that. By the end of the day, they will have climbed to their own heart's content, regardless of the name, grade, or length of the route. Most climbers, however, follow a more conventional path and keep to known routes of advertised grades, and use the book to match climb and grade to ability and inclination. A few seek out new routes and have a store of prospective names.

To sum up, then, guidebooks are not essential but they are more than useful – a lasting source of information and, possibly, of entertainment. Some of them are gems, to be cherished.

GRADING CLIMBS

There are as many systems of grading climbs as there are climbing countries, although, internally, most nations have, by now, settled on one system. The grade of difficulty of a particular climb or pitch is firstly a matter of the opinion of the first people who climbed it and, afterwards, a matter of consensus of all those who follow. The surprising aspect is not how often individuals disagree about the precise difficulty of a particular piece of rock, but how often they agree, and, indeed, how often that agreement is well-nigh universal.

The best way to show grading systems and how they compare across the world is by means of a chart, although, at best, this is an approximation. The Australian system is probably the most logical, progressing from 4 through to 30 on an open-ended scale (1 to 3 must be considered as walking). In theory, there can be 31, 32, 33, and more. How, though, is it possible to discern 30-odd grades of route? It is a finely tuned system. Many of the other methods are delightfully inconsistent. The British system is descriptive – up to Hard Very Severe – but it is hardly accurate, so that a 'difficult' would probably be a good choice for a first ever route and is, therefore, not really 'difficult' at all.

After that, the adjectives run out and the system begins again with 'E1', E for Extreme, which is also an open-ended system, currently resting at E8. The numerical suffixes give an indication of the technical difficulty of the climb. Originally designed for grading outcrop climbs of little or no seriousness, the system has been adopted nationally and is used in conjunction with the adjectival grading of a climb.

Nor is the American system logically unflawed. It has a straightforward, numerical progression from 5.0 through to 5.9 and then, at 5.10, alphabetical subdivisions 5.10a to 5.10d. The same subdivisions occur at 5.11 before the system again reverts to simple 5.12 and 5.13.

To begin with, it is probably a good idea to let discretion be the better part of your valour. Begin easily and modestly; you can always climb a harder route the next time. It is not so easy the other way around. For a very first route, go very carefully. That way you will gain a feel for the calibration of the grading scale. Some climbs may be disappointing but few in those early days are a waste of time. Similarly, when visiting a new area, it is no bad thing to aim low – there are some notorious local inconsistencies. For instance, there are 'Severes' at Sennen, a Cornish granite, coastal crag, which would rate 'VS' anywhere else in the land, while the denizens of the Peak District will tell you that any gritstone 'VS' is a Welsh 'E1' that some would rate even higher than that. The worrying thing is that, in some cases, they are right! European visitors to the United States are often stopped in their tracks and sometimes earlier than that – that is, before they have left the ground – by the legendary Yosemite off-widths, cracks that take some getting used to. Many never get used to them.

Europe's UIAA system was intended to be international but it has only met with intermittent acceptance. It is used mainly in the eastern Alps for mountain rock climbs, and for pitch gradings for climbs in the western Alps. On outcrops, [which include the 500-metre (1650-foot) cliffs of Verdon!] the

French use another scale (*see* the chart) and many other European countries have national scales of their own. There are even instances of grading systems that are unique to one crag. It is not as confusing as it sounds, however, and one or two samplers are usually enough to get the general feel of things.

GLOSSARY OF CLIFF FEATURES

amphitheatre a very large recess in the cliff face
arête a sharp rock feature rather like the outside corner of a building, a steep ridge
block a squarish lump of rock that may or may not be attached to the cliff
bulge a small overhang
buttress a very prominent section of the cliff
chimney a crack large enough to contain the entire body
chockstone a rock jammed in a crack
corner a feature rather like the inside corner of a building
flake a piece of rock that has peeled away or detached from the main face. A flake may vary in size from something the size of a thumbnail to a feature as big as the side of a house
glacis an easy-angled slab of rock
groove a shallow corner
gully a deep chasm usually running the entire length of the crag
ledge a flat area on the face. It can ber anything from a few centimetres to a few metres wide
niche a shallow, cave-like feature
off-width a crack that is too wide to hand jam but not wide enough to get into
overhang a roof of rock
overlap a small step in the continuity of the face
pedestal a flat-topped, detached pinnacle
pinnacle a detached feature rather like a church steeple
prow a feature rather like the prow of a ship
rib a prominent, slender feature – more rounded than an ARÊTE
scoop an indentation in the rock face, not as pronounced as a NICHE
spike a finger of rock

CHAPTER 9

ON GAMES CLIMBERS PLAY: AND OF ETHICS AND STYLE

Ethics '. . . actions which affect others in the climbing community . . .' Royal Robbins, leading Yosemite climber of the 1960s.

The game of climbing is played with more zest than most, but it is a game played without opponents, pitches, referees, crowds, or formal rules. But there are rules, of a sort; rules which climbers, rather grandly, call ethics, perhaps because climbers like to cast themselves on an anarchic stage and find the word 'rules' hard to stomach. The interesting thing about climbing ethics is that, although they have never been set out, and although they are certainly not promoted, most climbers are aware, feel perhaps, what they are – even if they cheerfully transgress them.

It is not easy to explain these ethics to a newcomer. Nor is it easy to explain why they exist. Two very different explanations from very different sources might help to illuminate the labyrinthine ethical corridors of this sport of no rules. First Dennis Kemp, a respected and redoubtable British climbing veteran, in his excellent little handbook *Rock Climbing* (Know the Game Series) says, by way of an explanation of ethics:

There is this climb in Wales that I would like to lead so very much. It has the reputation of being very good; everyone of note has done it; it is very hard and really out of my class. I am not climbing that well yet, but one day I hope to have a go, to enjoy the climbing but also to enjoy saying to my friends, when asked, 'Yes, I've done Vector.'

I have in fact done the climb, leading through with a skilled friend, leaving him to do the long and hard middle pitch. But that is not the same as leading it. I did have a go at leading the middle pitch, but failed halfway. So I know where the climb goes, what the moves are like. You traverse

to the right to where you can get a good spike runner, then go up on small steep holds to gain the 'Ochre Slab' where there is a peg you can clip another runner to. Then steeply up the slab to arrive breathless in a small cave with umpteen pegs where you can make a belay and take a stance. When I was seconding, I got gripped on the Ochre Slab and held on to the peg. This is 'using aid'.

Can I claim to have done the climb properly, even seconding? I could make the climb even easier by holding on to more of the runners my leader had put in. Would it be OK to do this? Could I also call for help from a tight top rope? Does one not have to draw a line somewhere? Could I still say I had climbed Vector if I got a long ladder and shinned up that to the cave stance?

My view is that I can climb the route absolutely any way I like from a long builders' ladder to the sneakiest tweak on a sling when no-one is looking, if that is what I want and it gives me pleasure, provided I do not then go and claim I had 'climbed' Vector. That would be cheating. Unethical. I want to gain the respect of my mates, not lose it. And there is no point in cheating to impress my neighbours who do not climb. They do not know the difference between Vector and Flying Buttress – they would probably be more impressed at the latter because it is longer and on a mountain. So the ethical thing is to be absolutely honest and say, 'I failed on Vector – did the route but had to pull up on the peg'. Now, when I fell off that time it was because I dithered on one small and greasy finger-hold. I would not trust myself to it, and ran out of cool and fell off. Would I be justified in taking a hammer and chipping away at the rock to improve the hold? The answer to

this is very clear; never. By all means climb the rock in any manner that pleases you, but never at the expense of damaging or changing the route for others.

Ah, but what about using chalk on that greasy hold? That does not damage or change the route for others? But it does, you know. For one thing, chalked-up holds are just plain ugly. And no scope is left for route-finding. Searching out the holds to use is part of the enjoyment and skill of rock climbing. Use chalk on your fingers if you must, but get it on the rock and it is an action that affects others in the climbing community. Unethical.

Talking of damage, consider now the question of pegs. Hammer a peg into a crack so small you cannot ever use it as a handhold, and you have an anchor for a belay. The second man can take the peg out, leaving the rock as you found it. But not quite. Putting the peg in and bashing it out damages and widens the crack, leaving an unsightly scar. On popular routes this scarring and widening becomes very pronounced and can change the route completely.

The modern ethic is quite simple: Do not use pegs, use nut runners instead. However, it is quite ethical and often the only thing to do – to use pegs for belaying, particularly when they are in place. Do not use aid. Climb a route until you can push it no farther then either reverse down or abseil off. If you use any aid you cannot claim the route.

This stringent, modern ethic is quite demanding and is not helped by guidebooks always being something like ten years behind the times. Points of aid are

---

Abseiling to inspect a climb prior to making the first ascent. Arguable tactics?

mentioned frequently in route decriptions, but standards and techniques have advanced since then. Also, the use of nuts had not reached today's level, and where a guidebook says 'peg runner' or 'peg belay' you can usually get one or more nuts in instead.

I think it is significant, too, that the modern young ethical hard climbers also tend to be on the side of 'Friends of the Earth' taking 'do nothing to harm the rock' to mean 'do nothing to harm the environment'. This has many implications, from carrying your own litter away from the crag rather than leaving it there under a stone, to tidying up other people's rubbish because it is offensive to the eye and detracts from the pleasure of being there. From walking an extra distance from your parked car to a crag to avoid nuisance to local residents, to leaving any barn you bivvy in absolutely spotless.

This sums up the ethical debate rather nicely. An interesting thing is that, since Dennis wrote that in 1975, the climbing world has adjusted the 'rules' somewhat in that strange way that the climbing world does these things – a sort of process of subliminal concensus. Chalk is now 'in'; great white clouds of it. Those who objected to it on the grounds explained above, have seen their objections swept aside by a welter of climbers who, on discovering that chalk gave them a better chance and made things easier, allowed their ambition to triumph over their concern for ethics. Or perhaps they did not recognize those ethics in the first place. Or they did not care. Anyway, most of us now use chalk, wilfully. So chalk, for the moment and for the forseeable future, is in, is ethical – or, at least, is no longer unethical. Pegs though, are all but 'out' – in Britain and in the United States, anyway. You would probably get away with a few pegs, preferably at belays, on a

The tools of the prior inspectionist, a wire brush, hammer and lots of runners to pre place. Arguable tactics.

new 'E7', but you would never be forgiven for hammering one into a new 'Severe', or an old climb of any grade, for any purpose. Bolts are a bit more ambiguous. At the moment, in Britain, they are drilled fairly indiscriminately into limestone and slate, for runners and belays on hard, new routes – say, 'E3' and upwards. Often they are pre-placed by abseil. The climbing world is currently trying to resolve what will be the ethics of all this. A second stab at British ethics was recently taken by Malcolm Campbell who tabulated British climbing ethics by the following set of 'rules':

1. First ascents may involve minimum 'cleaning' of vegetation and genuinely loose rock from abseil. 'Chipping' of holds is not permitted and the pre-placing of runners is also frowned upon.

2. The use of pegs should be kept to an absolute minimum.

3. Expansion bolts should never be placed on traditional, volcanic mountain rock, sandstone, or gritstone. Their use on limestone and other softer rock such as slate should be seen as a last resort.

4. Chalk should be used conservatively, and only when needed.

5. When repeating routes, the style to aim for is 'on-sight, no falls, no rests'.

6. In the event of a fall (or a 'technical' fall, such as grabbing a runner), the climber should immediately lower down to the first place where he or she can 'rest' without aid from the rope, before climbing back up to attempt the moves again.

7. Hanging from the rope after a fall before continuing is called 'hang-dogging', and is tantamount to artificial climbing. Falling and lowering from progressively higher runners

is called 'yo-yoing', and is another form of cheating.

He went on to add:

In an attempt to establish a clearer ethic, some climbers are adopting the French 'Red-Point' technique which allows any amount of 'rule-bending' whilst the climber 'practises', as long as he or she eventually makes a 'red-point' ascent with no falls, and no weight placed on any runners. Time only will determine whether or not this ethic replaces the 'on-sight' one, but it seems that the idea of starting at the bottom and climbing to the top is losing out to the 'Clean, Inspect, Practise then Climb' School. But the only thing which is certain is that the game will evolve, and evolution means change.

So far two categories of ethic emerge: the personal performance ethic and the environmental ethic. Of these, it could be argued that the first matters only if it matters to you and the second matters if it matters to others.

At last the climber has a number of choices:

1. Stick to the rules where possible (and where you can identify them!).

2. Bend the rules to suit – that is, to succeed.

3. Claim to be sticking to the rules but in fact bending them – that is, cheating.

4. Ignore all the rules and do your own thing.

Most climbers seem happy to follow choice **1.** most of the time, which is as well because anarchy is never too far around the corner of the climbing game.

If your understanding of ethics is still incomplete, do not worry.

'Kirkus Climb' a classic route for beginners. On such a climb the ethics are in no doubt, climb as it was first ascended, with rope, runners, and pleasure.

TERMINOLOGY

There are certain idiosyncrasies in climbing terminology peculiar to different parts of the world.

The differences are not really significant, but visitors to the United States may find the following terminology helpful.

USA	'ENGLISH TERM'
RAPPEL	ABSEIL
BINERS	KARABINERS
PINS	PITONS
LIEBACK	LAYBACK
STEMMING	BRIDGING
DIHEDRAL	CORNER or OPEN GROOVE
KNICKERS	BREECHES
HIKE	WALK TO CLIMB
'UP ROPE'	'TAKE IN'
'OFF BELAY'	'SAFE'
OUTSIDE CORNER	ARETE
INSIDE CORNER	CORNER

Throughout this book the 'English' versions of these terms have been used.

FURTHER READING

MAGAZINES AND PERIODICALS
Alpinisme et Randonée (France)
Ascent (International)
Climber (British)
Climbing (United States)
Extrem (Spanish)
High (British)
The Iwa to Yuki (Japan)
Mountain Magazine (International)
Rock and Ice (United States)
Vertical (France)
Wild (Australia)

TECHNICAL MANUALS
Ashton, Steve. *Scrambling.*
MacInnes, Hamish. *International Mountain Rescue Handbook.*
New Zealand Mountain Safety Council, *Mountaincraft.*
Scott, Doug. *Big Wall Climbing.*
Shepherd, Nigel. 1987. *Self Rescue Techniques for Climbers and Instructors.* Adventure Unlimited, Dolwyddelan.
Sierra Club Books. *The Climbers' Handbook*, USA.

Wilkerson, James. *Medicine for Mountaineers*

GENERAL ILLUSTRATED BOOKS
Jones, Chris. *Climbing in North America.*
Edlinger, Patrick *et al* (Featuring.) *Operata Verticale. Climbing in the Verdon.*
Friend, Joe. *Rock Climbs of Australia.*
Mountaineers, The. *Mountaineering: The Freedom of the Hills.* Seattle.
Mountain Magazine. With an Introduction by Terry King. *World Climbing.*
Newman, Bernard (Ed.). *Extreme Rock.*
Pause and Winkler. *Extreme Alpine Rock.*
Radcliffe, Peter. *Land of Mountains.*
Roper, Steve and Steck, Allen. *Fifty Classic Climbs of North America.*
Wilson, Ken (Ed.). *Hard Rock.*

GUIDEBOOKS

It is impossible to list guidebooks to the world's climbing areas. There are hundreds, even thousands of them. The following list of addresses will be found useful if you need to know about the guidebooks available in a particular country.

CANADA
Alpine Club of Canada
PO Box 1026
Banff
Alberta TOL OCO

FRANCE
Federation Français de la Montagne
Rue La Boetie
75008 Paris

GERMANY
Deutscher Alpenverein
Praterinsel 5
8 München 22.

BRITAIN
British Mountaineering Council
Crawford House
Booth Street East
Manchester M13 9RZ

ITALY
Club Alpino Italiano
Via Ugo Foscolo 3
20121 Milano

JAPAN
Japanese Mountaineering Association
c/o Japan Amateur Sports Association
11-1 Jinnan
Shibuya-Ku
Tokyo
150

NEW ZEALAND
New Zealand Alpine Club
PO Box 41-038
Eastbourne

SPAIN
Federacion Espanola de Montanismo
Alberto Aguilera 3-4
Madrid 15

UNITED STATES
American Alpine Club
113 East 90th Street
New York
NY 10028

INDEX

DEDICATION

This book is dedicated to all our friends.

We would like to thank all those who have helped, in any way, for their kind assistance.
In particular Wild Country, whose generosity in supplying equipment was much appreciated,
and the Joe Brown climbing shop in Capel Curig and Climber and Rambler of Betws y Coed,
for the loan of equipment for photographs.
Finally, a special thanks to Mike Woolridge for producing such excellent drawings.

John Barry.   Nigel Shepherd.   January 1988.

PRINTED IN BELGIUM BY

proost

INTERNATIONAL BOOK PRODUCTION